Tucholsky Wagner Zola Scott Sydow Freud Schlegel
Turgenev Wallace Fonatne
Twain Walther von der Vogelweide Fouqué Friedrich II. von Preußen
Weber Freiligrath Frey
Fechner Fichte Weiße Rose von Fallersleben Kant Ernst Frommel
Richthofen
Engels Fielding Hölderlin
Fehrs Faber Flaubert Eichendorff Tacitus Dumas
Eliasberg Ebner Eschenbach
Feuerbach Maximilian I. von Habsburg Fock Zweig Eliot
Ewald Vergil
Goethe London
Mendelssohn Balzac Shakespeare Elisabeth von Österreich Dostojewski Ganghofer
Trackl Lichtenberg Rathenau Doyle Gjellerup
Stevenson Hambruch
Mommsen Tolstoi Lenz Droste-Hülshoff
Thoma Hanrieder
Dach Verne von Arnim Hägele Hauff Humboldt
Reuter Hagen Hauptmann Gautier
Karrillon Rousseau
Garschin Defoe Hebbel Baudelaire
Damaschke Descartes
Hegel Kussmaul Herder
Wolfram von Eschenbach Dickens Schopenhauer Rilke George
Bronner Darwin Melville Grimm Jerome
Campe Horváth Aristoteles Bebel Proust
Bismarck Vigny Barlach Voltaire Federer Herodot
Gengenbach Heine
Storm Casanova Tersteegen Grillparzer Georgy
Chamberlain Lessing Langbein Gilm Gryphius
Brentano Lafontaine
Strachwitz Claudius Schiller Kralik Iffland Sokrates
Katharina II. von Rußland Bellamy Schilling
Gerstäcker Raabe Gibbon Tschechow
Löns Hesse Hoffmann Gogol Wilde Vulpius
Luther Heym Hofmannsthal Klee Hölty Morgenstern Gleim
Roth Heyse Klopstock Kleist Goedicke
Luxemburg Puschkin Homer Mörike
Machiavelli La Roche Horaz Musil
Navarra Aurel Musset Kierkegaard Kraft Kraus
Lamprecht Kind Kirchhoff Hugo Moltke
Nestroy Marie de France
Laotse Ipsen Liebknecht
Nietzsche Nansen
Marx Ringelnatz
von Ossietzky Lassalle Gorki Klett Leibniz
May vom Stein Lawrence Irving
Petalozzi Knigge
Platon Kafka
Sachs Pückler Michelangelo Kock
Poe Liebermann Korolenko
de Sade Praetorius Mistral Zetkin

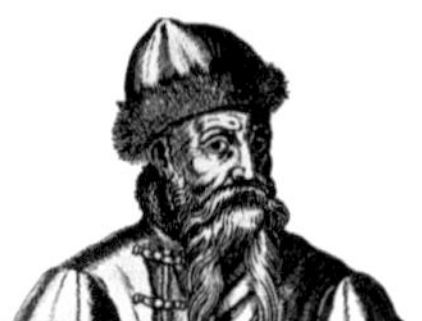

The publishing house tredition has created the series **TREDITION CLASSICS**. It contains classical literature works from over two thousand years. Most of these titles have been out of print and off the bookstore shelves for decades.

The book series is intended to preserve the cultural legacy and to promote the timeless works of classical literature. As a reader of a **TREDITION CLASSICS** book, the reader supports the mission to save many of the amazing works of world literature from oblivion.

The symbol of **TREDITION CLASSICS** is Johannes Gutenberg (1400 – 1468), the inventor of movable type printing.

With the series, tredition intends to make thousands of international literature classics available in printed format again – worldwide.

All books are available at book retailers worldwide in paperback and in hardcover. For more information please visit: www.tredition.com

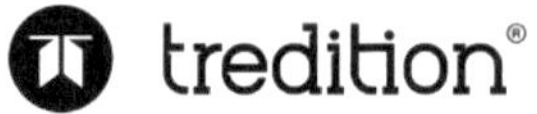

tredition was established in 2006 by Sandra Latusseck and Soenke Schulz. Based in Hamburg, Germany, tredition offers publishing solutions to authors and publishing houses, combined with worldwide distribution of printed and digital book content. tredition is uniquely positioned to enable authors and publishing houses to create books on their own terms and without conventional manufacturing risks.

For more information please visit: www.tredition.com

Bell's Cathedrals: The Priory Church of St. Bartholomew-the-Great, Smithfield A Short History of the Foundation and a Description of the Fabric and also of the Church of St. Bartholomew-the-Less

George Worley

Imprint

This book is part of the TREDITION CLASSICS series.

Author: George Worley
Cover design: toepferschumann, Berlin (Germany)

Publisher: tredition GmbH, Hamburg (Germany)
ISBN: 978-3-8495-0725-1

www.tredition.com
www.tredition.de

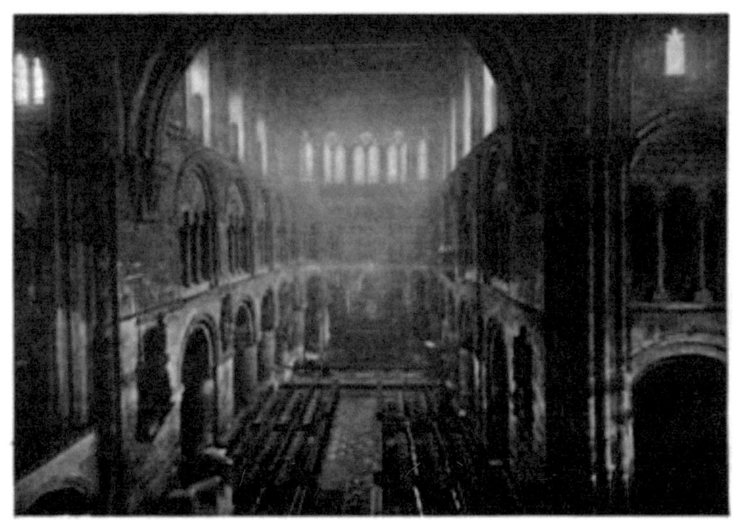

THE INTERIOR FROM THE ORGAN GALLERY.

PREFACE

v In gathering material for this handbook I have received valuable help from several friends, whose kindness calls for grateful recognition. My thanks are due, in the first place, to the Rev. W. F. G. Sandwith, Rector of St. Bartholomew-the-Great, and the lay custodians of the church, for the facilities which have allowed me to examine the building in all its parts, and for the readiness with which they have given information, not accessible elsewhere, on various points of its history and architecture. In this matter, besides more personal obligations, I feel that I owe much, in common with many others, to Mr. E. A. Webb, the active member of the Restoration Committee, for the suggestive data of his open lectures, and for the interesting expositions of the fabric by which he has always supplemented them. Others to whom I am indebted are Dom Henry Norbert Birt, O.S.B., of Downside Abbey, and Mr. Charles W. F. Goss, Librarian to the Bishopsgate Institute, for their skilful guidance in the literature of the subject; Mr. F. C. Eeles, Secretary to the Alcuin Club, for the Elizabethan Inventory and account of the Mediaeval Bells; and Messrs. Wm. Hill and Son, the famous builders, for particulars of the organ.

For the illustration of the book, Mr. A. Russell Baker has kindly contributed a selection from his rare set of old engravings, before presenting the whole to St. Bartholomew's Hospital.

vi The photographic views of the church and monuments, as seen at the present day, were taken by Mr. Edgar Scamell, of 120, Crouch Hill; and the seal-impressions by Mr. A. P. Ready, the British Museum artist. Finally, Sir Aston Webb, R.A., has to be thanked for the ground-plans of the church and monastic buildings; and Mr. G. H. Smith for the plan and dimensions of St. Bartholomew-the-Less.

A list of books and papers is appended for the benefit of students anxious for more detailed information than could be included here.

G. W.

June, 1908 vii

A SELECTION OF WORKS ON ST. BARTHOLO-MEW-THE-GREAT

"The Book of the Foundation of St. Bartholomew's Church in London, sometime belonging to the Priory of the same in West Smithfield." Edited from the original manuscript, with an Introduction and Notes by Norman Moore, M.D. 1885.

"The Charter of King Henry I to St. Bartholomew's Priory, addressed to the Archbishop of Canterbury and to Gilbert the Universal, Bishop of London, in the year 1133." Edited with Notes, from the copy in the Record Office, by Norman Moore, M.D. 1891.

"Rahere's Charter of 1137." Translated, with Explanatory Notes, by Norman Moore, M.D. 1904.

"The Ordinance of Richard de Ely, Bishop of London, as to St. Bartholomew's Priory in West Smithfield, witnessed by Henry Fitzailwin, First Mayor of London, in the year 1198." Edited from the original document by Norman Moore, M.D. 1886.

viii Dugdale's "Monasticon Anglicanum" (edit. Bandinel, Caley, and Sir Henry Ellis) is indispensable to the student. The sixth volume (p. 291 *sqq.*) contains an account of the Smithfield Foundation, and (p. 37 *sqq.*) the Rule for Austin Canons. For the latter the reader will do well to consult also R. Duellius' "Antiqua Statuta Canonicorum S. Augustini metrice cum glossulis optimis," and "Regula Canonicorum Regularium per Hugonem de S. Victore Commentario declarata."

For illustrative matter during the Tudor period reference may be made to "The Elizabethan Religious Settlement," by Dom Henry Norbert Birt, O.S.B., 1907; the Rev. C. F. Raymund Palmer's "Articles, chiefly on the Friars Preachers of England, reprinted from archaeological journals, 1878-85"; and "Obituary Notices of the Friars Preachers or Dominicans of the English Province." 1884.

The literary work of Fr. Perrin (the Marian Prior) is described in Charles Dodd's "Church History of England" (1727 edition), and Pit's "De Illust. Scriptoribus Angliae."

Besides the invaluable "Historia Anglorum" of Matthew Paris (ed. Sir F. Madden), and Stow's "Survey of London" (ed. John Strype), the following books may be found useful:

"Repertorium, or History of the Diocese of London." Richard Newcourt. 1708.

"New View of London." Edward Hatton. 1708.

"New Remarks of London: by the Company of Parish Clerks." 1732.

"London and its Environs described." R. and J. Dodsley. 1761.

"History of London." Win. Maitland. (Ed. Entick, 1772.)

"Londinium Redivivum." J. P. Malcolm. 1803.

"Londina Illustrata." Robert Wilkinson. 1819.

"The Churches of London." G. Godwin and J. Britton. 1839.

"Memories of Bartholomew Fair." H. Morley. 1859.

ix The progress of the modern work at the church has been announced from time to time in the circulars issued by the Restoration Committee, the substance of which is incorporated in the text, where also the other authorities consulted by the present writer are referred to.

CONTENTS

xi

LIST OF ILLUSTRATIONS

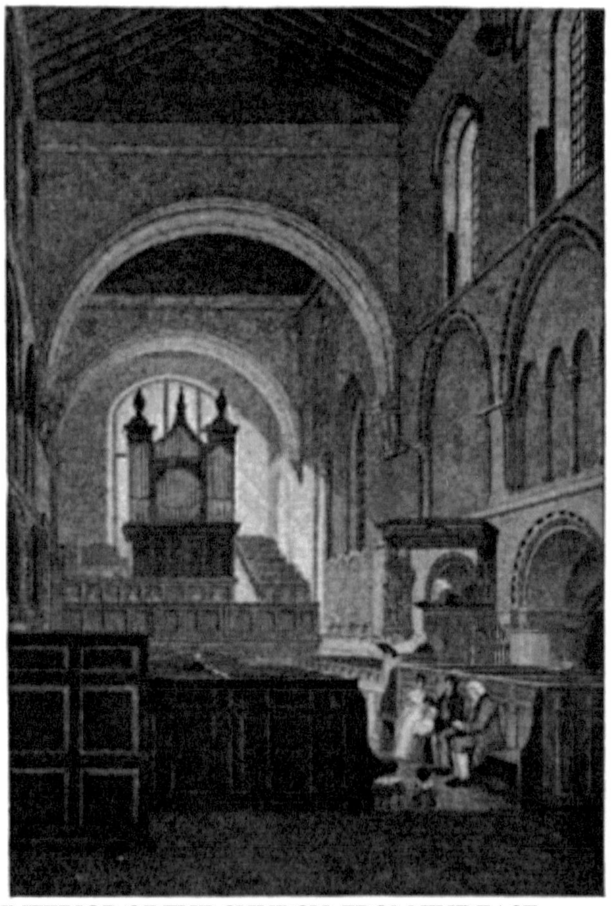

INTERIOR OF THE CHURCH, FROM THE EAST
From a print of 1805.

ST. BARTHOLOMEW-THE-GREAT

CHAPTER I

HISTORY

The spring and fountain-head of our information about the Priory of St. Bartholomew-the-Great is an account of the foundation, interwoven with the life and miracles of Rahere, the founder, which was written in Latin by one of the Canons soon after Rahere's death in the reign of Henry II. An illuminated copy of this work, made at the end of the fourteenth century, is preserved in the British Museum, with an English translation, which forms the groundwork of all subsequent histories. [1]

4 Allowing for a few contradictory dates and statements in this precious document, and for the occasional flights of a pious imagination in the biographer or his subject, we arrive at the following historical basis: Rahere was a man of humble origin, who had found his way to the Court of Henry I, where he won favour by his agreeable manners and witty conversation, rendered piquant, as it appears, by a certain flavouring of licentiousness, and took a prominent part in arranging the music, plays, and other entertainments in which the King and his courtiers delighted during the first part of the reign. [2]

In the year 1120 a total change was wrought in Henry's character by the loss of his only legitimate son in the wreck of the "White Ship," on its voyage from Normandy to England, after which the King is said never to have smiled again. The event naturally cast a gloom over the Court; frivolities were abandoned, and religious devotion, either genuine or assumed in polite acquiescence with the royal humour, took the place of the amusements which had hitherto held sway. In one case, at least, the spirit of reformation was at work in good earnest. Rahere, repenting of his wasted life, thereupon started on a pilgrimage to Rome, to do penance for his sins on the ground hallowed by the martyrdom of St. Paul, some three miles from the city. The spot known as the Three Fountains, now rendered more or less sanitary by the free planting of eucalyptus, was then and long afterwards particularly unhealthy, and while there Rahere was attacked by malarial fever. In his distress he made a vow that, if he were spared, he would establish a hospital for the poor, as a thank-offering, on his return to England.

5 His prayer was granted, but his recovery was slow. During his convalescence he had a vision, or dream, in which he thought a winged monster had seized him in its claws, and was about to drop him into a bottomless pit, when a majestic form came to his rescue, and thus addressed him: "I am Bartholomew, the Apostle of Jesus Christ, that come to succour thee in thine anguish, and to open to thee the secret mysteries of heaven. Know me truly, by the will and commandment of the Holy Trinity, and the common favour of the celestial court and council, to have chosen a place in the suburbs of London, at Smithfield, where in my name thou shall found a church. This spiritual house Almighty God shall inhabit, and hallow it, and glorify it. Wherefore doubt thou nought; only give thy diligence, and my part shall be to provide necessaries, direct, build, and end this work." [3] Rahere at once promised compliance, and, as soon as he got back to London, first obtained the King's consent, and then, "nothing omitting of care and diligence, two works of piety began, one for the vow that he had made, the other as to him by precept was enjoined." [4]

The suburb of Smithfield (Smoothfield) is said to have already occurred to Edward the Confessor as a suitable place for a church on the outskirts of London, possibly as affording a similar area, in its level and marshy surface, to that chosen for his Abbey at Westminster. The greater part of it was, indeed, covered by water, the one dry spot (known as "The Elms") being reserved for public executions, which continued to take place there till some centuries later. The eastern portion of this waste land was granted by Henry I, through the agency of Richard de Belmeis, Bishop of London; and it was here that, in the year 1123, Rahere began building. [5]

In a marvellously short time the funds were forthcoming, and his double object was achieved in the erection of the Hospital, with the Church at a little distance, the whole being dedicated by the same friendly bishop to St. Bartholomew the Apostle, in fulfilment of Rahere's vow and the Saint's instructions.

Rahere is said to have been assisted in his architectural work by Alfune, who had founded St. Giles's Church, Cripplegate, in the year 1090; and there is a story to the effect that three noble travellers, or merchants, from Byzantium were present at the foundation, when they foretold its future greatness, and were consulted by Rahere as to the design and character of the building while his plans were under consideration.

6 On the southern side of the church the group of buildings gradually arose which constituted the Priory, of which the founder, having devoted himself to the monastic life, of course became the first Prior; and here he spent the rest of his days with thirteen companions—the sub-prior and twelve subordinates—all living under the Rule of the Canons Regular of St. Augustine. The number was afterwards brought up to thirty-five by Thomas of St. Osyth, the second Prior (1144-1174), who made a corresponding addition to the premises. [6]

In 1133, when the buildings were fairly advanced, and the value of Rahere's work had got to be recognized, a charter of privileges was granted by Henry I to the Prior and Canons. Commencing with an invocation of the Holy Trinity, it was addressed to the Archbishop of Canterbury and the Bishop of London, with a greeting to all the King's faithful subjects, especially the citizens of London. Its comprehensive immunities may be inferred from the opening paragraph:

7

Know ye that I have granted, and have by this my charter confirmed, to the Church of St. Bartholomew of London, and to Rahere the Prior, and to the Canons Regular, in the same church serving God, and to the poor of the Hospital of the same church, that they be free from all earthly servitude, and all earthly power and subjection, except episcopal customs, to wit, only consecration of the church, baptism, and ordination of clergy; and that as any church in all England is free, so this church be free, and all lands to it appertaining, which it now has, or which Rahere the Prior, or the Canons, may be able reasonably to acquire, whether by purchase or by gift. And it shall have socc and sac, and thol and theme, and infogheneteof; and all liberties and free customs and acquittances in all things which belong to the same church in wood and in plain, in meadows and pastures, in waters and mills, in ways and paths, in pools and vineyards, and marshes and fisheries, and in all places now and for ever. [7]

Another paragraph may be worth quoting, as it expressly includes Bartholomew Fair among the privileges conveyed, though it is clear from the terms of the instrument that a fair had previously been held in the open space at Smithfield on the Saint's anniversary. Even before the accession of Henry I there had been a market on the spot, known as "the King's Market" when the ground was allotted to Rahere. (*Vide* "Vetusta Monumenta," vol. ii.)

I grant also my firm peace to all persons coming to and returning from the fair which is wont to be celebrated in that place at the Feast of St. Bartholomew; and I forbid any one of the royal officials to send to implead any one, or without the consent of the Canons on those three days — to wit, the eve of the feast, the feast itself, and the day following — to demand customary dues from them.

8 The observance was afterwards extended to a double octave of fourteen days, and included all kinds of shows and entertainments, theatrical, conjuring, and acrobatic performances, in addition to the traffic in cloth-stuffs, horses and cattle, which gave the fair its commercial importance. The stalls, or booths, in which the portable goods were exposed for sale, were held within the monastery walls, the gates of which were locked at night, and a watch kept over the enclosure. [8]

Rahere died on 20th September, 1144, and was buried in the church, where his tomb occupies the usual place for Founders on the north side of the sanctuary, surrounded by his magnificent Norman work in the choir, with the ambulatory beyond it, and extending upwards to the arcading of the triforium. The eastern part of the clerestory is a modern reproduction of that which superseded Rahere's; but, with this exception, the interior of the choir was probably much the same originally as it is (restored) to-day.

There was, however, a central tower, and, if the design on the twelfth-century Priory seal is to be trusted, a high circular turret at each end of the exterior. [9]

9 Thomas of St. Osyth, the second Prior (d. 1174), erected the transepts and the easternmost bays of the nave, all of which bear signs of the architectural transition. The nave was probably completed during the next half-century, in the Early-English (then superseding the heavier Norman) style, as may be inferred from the surviving western gateway, and the mutilated columns which remain within the building at the western end.

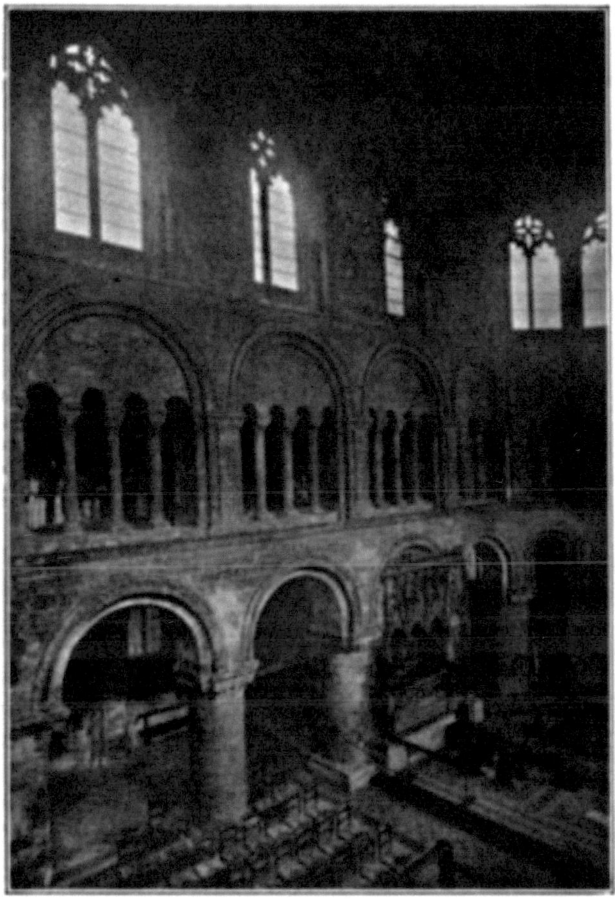

THE NORTH SIDE OF THE CHOIR FROM THE TRIFORIUM

10 Perpendicular work was introduced early in the fifteenth century, when Roger de Walden, Bishop of London (1405-1406), built a chantry-chapel to the north-east of the choir, and inserted a new clerestory, in the then fashionable style, in place of the original. He also made a considerable alteration in the chancel by substituting a square east-end for the circular apse, part of which was taken down and used as building material for the innovation. But de Walden's work was cut short by his death, when he had scarcely held the See of London for two years, and was buried in his Chapel at St. Bartholomew's, instead of in the Cathedral Church like most of his predecessors.

The Lady Chapel, with the crypt beneath it, dates from about 1410, when also the central tower was probably rebuilt, and decorative additions were made to the Founder's tomb, in the shape of a canopy and panelling. In the first part of the next century Prior Bolton (1505-32) inserted the Oriel window on the southern side of the choir-triforium and the doorway in the south ambulatory, both of which bear his sculptured rebus—a *bolt*, or arrow, driven through a *tun*. In 1539 his successor, Robert Fuller, the last of the Augustinian Priors, surrendered the entire property to Henry VIII, in compliance with the Act of Dissolution, its value having been already ascertained in the twenty-sixth year of the King's reign. The exact figures are given by Dugdale as follows:

Summa	totalis	hujus monasterii.	£773	0s.	1¾d.
"	"	reprisarum	£79	10s.	3½d.
		Et remanet clare	£693	9s.	10¼d.

11

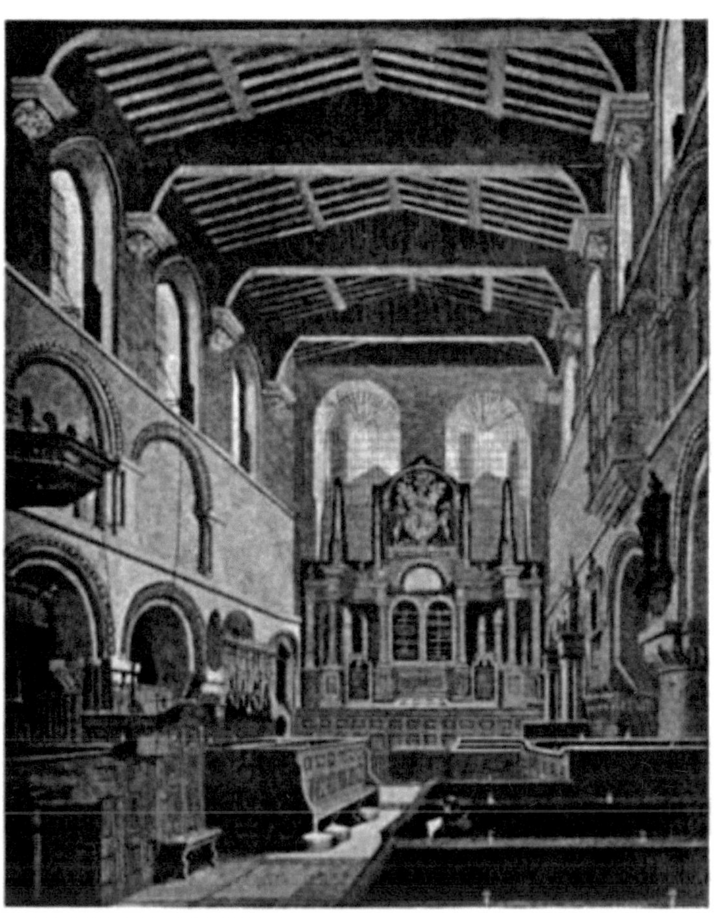

INTERIOR OF THE CHOIR
From a print of 1822

12 For many years before the dissolution of the monasteries the system on which they rested had been gradually undermined by the spread of the Reformation, accompanied by a growing conviction that the religious communities had not only outlived their usefulness, and to a great extent departed from the high standard of their founders, but that their enormous wealth had given them an influence far beyond that of any other institution, or combination of institutions, in the kingdom, and brought them into formidable

rivalry with the State itself—the more dangerous in proportion to their devoted adherence to the Papacy, with which the State was in collision. By whatever unworthy motives Henry VIII may have been governed in aiming at the monastic property, he was therefore able to bring forward many political considerations, which coincided with those arising out of religious doctrines, to make his measures intelligible to his people, and consequently easy to himself. Among the various plausible reasons which were urged against the continued existence of the conventual houses, one of the most likely to appeal to the practical sense of the multitude was the misuse of the resources with which they had been endowed. While it was admitted that in their earlier days they had been extremely useful in mitigating distress among the poor, it was now argued that their indiscriminate charities were doing more harm than good, and that the changed economic conditions of the sixteenth century called for a corresponding change in the distribution of relief, to save the country from being overrun by undeserving mendicants, amongst whom some of the religious Orders were themselves to be reckoned. It does not appear that any part of this argument held good against the Augustinian Canons, or that the more serious moral charges brought against the smaller communities were at all applicable to their case, which was rather one of involvement in a common ruin than the result of any specific accusation. It is true there are instances of laxity at individual houses, showing a too easy discipline where they occurred, but there is nothing sufficiently extensive or important to compromise the Order as a whole, or materially damage its character in the eyes of the impartial modern student. [10]

13 It might have been expected that some immunity from the wholesale spoliation which followed the Act would have been granted to Rahere's foundation, in view of his special provision for the poor in the hospital which was an integral part of it. The hospital has indeed been allowed to survive as a separate institution; but the whole of the strictly monastic buildings were doomed, the nave of the church being at once pulled down, and the choir only preserved for the use of the parish. With this reservation, the site of the Priory and the buildings upon it, including the Lady Chapel, were sold in 1546 to Sir Richard Rich, Knight (Attorney General), for the consideration of £1,064 11*s.* 3*d.*, and the property has remained in

the hands of his descendants till quite recent years. The possession was, however, interrupted by Queen Mary, who introduced the Dominican Order of Black Friars into the Convent. They had started rebuilding the nave when the accession of Elizabeth meant a return to the policy of her father, the expulsion of the friars, and the restitution of the Priory estate to Richard (then Lord) Rich and his heirs "in free socage," by a renewal of the previous grant. [11]

14 Some idea of the strong ecclesiastical influence broken up at the Dissolution may be gathered from a glance at any old map of London, showing the numerous religious foundations by which the Priory was then surrounded, now for the most part swept away, or only surviving here and there in institutions which retain the ancient names under modern conditions. Immediately to the north lay the Carthusian monastery, familiarly known as the Charterhouse. On the north-west was the Priory of St. John-of-Jerusalem, founded by the Knights Hospitallers. The Franciscan Convent of the Grey Friars extended along the southern boundary of St. Bartholomew's, between the Priory walls and St. Paul's Cathedral. To the south-west, near the Thames, there was the monastery of the Carmelites, or White Friars, with the church and houses of the Knights Templars beyond it. Within the City, to the east, were the great establishments of the Austin Friars and St. Helen's nunnery, while east and west the churches spread—many of monastic origin—culminating in two of the most important buildings in Europe, the Tower of London and the palace of Westminster, each with its ecclesiastical dependencies, the whole dominated by the mediaeval spirit about to be dispelled, for good or evil, by the great movements of the Renaissance and Reformation.

A conjectural restoration of the Priory buildings, as they stood in Prior Bolton's time, based on the records available in 1893, and the architectural fragments which then remained, shows them to have been bounded on the northern side by the Church, which extended from the Lady Chapel at its eastern extremity to somewhere near the line indicated by the small archway now leading from the public square into the churchyard on the west. This churchyard covers the ground formerly occupied by the nave, a mutilated portion of which remains within the building, attached to the lower stage of the central tower. It seems clear that the choir once extended over the tower-space, and was separated from the nave by a screen, with a parish-altar on its western side for public worship, while the chancel was reserved for the monastic services, with a raised presbytery for the high altar at its eastern end—a threefold division providing for the ancient ritual arrangement.

In the ambulatory on the northern side of the choir there were apparently three chapels, besides Bishop Walden's chantry, which was the easternmost of the series, and is supposed to have had a semicircular apse. There was a similar, but rather smaller, chapel opposite to it on the south side, and between it and the south transept a sacristy, erected about 1350.

Outside the Lady Chapel lay the cemetery of the Canons, on the favourite (south) side for burials. The cloister formed a large quadrangle attached to the south aisle. The Prior's residence was probably on the western side of the quadrangle, and on the south there was a range of buildings comprising the refectory, buttery, and kitchen, with the Close beyond them.

15 Opening into the cloister on the east was the Chapter House, an oblong structure, adjoining which, on the south, was the dormitory, overlooking the Mulberry Gardens on the east, and the Close on its western side. [12]

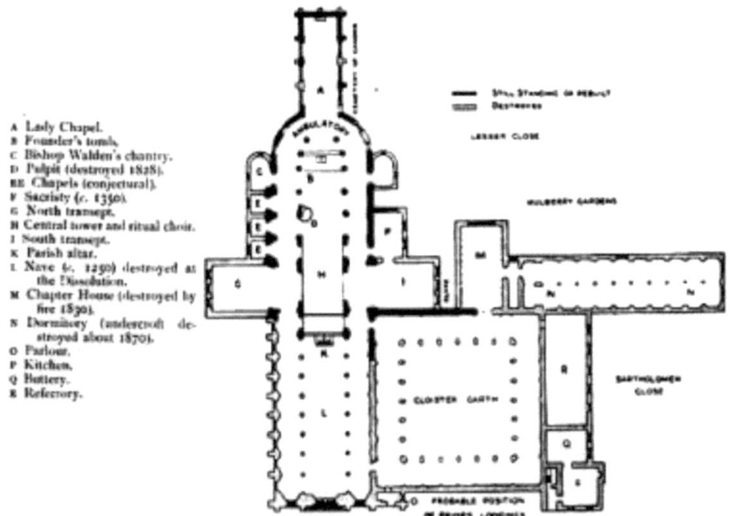

PLAN, PARTLY CONJECTURAL, OF THE MONASTIC BUILD-
INGS AT THE DISSOLUTION

16 The work of demolition commenced immediately after the transfer of the property to Henry VIII, when the nave was destroyed; and as soon as Sir Richard Rich came into possession, he started pulling down the buildings for the sake of the materials, which were used in the erection of new houses where the old had formerly stood, as well as on the gardens and orchards around them. By the time of Queen Elizabeth the district had become a favourite residential quarter for great people, who gradually disappeared with the growth of London, and the migration of gentry westwards, when the houses vacated in Smithfield were let off in tenements to the same sort of poor people who now share the neighbourhood with merchants and shopkeepers.

During Elizabeth's reign the church had been allowed to get into a very dilapidated state, and that it was in some danger of total destruction appears from a letter written by Edmund Grindal in 1563, while he was Bishop of London, to Sir William Cecil, proposing to take the lead from the roof, and transfer it to St. Paul's Cathedral:

St. Bartholomew's Churche, adjoining to my L. Rich's house, is in decaye, and so increaseth dailye. It hath an heavie coate of lead, wch wolde doe a verie goode service for the Mother Churche of Powles. I have obtayned my L. Rich's goode wishes, and if I coulde obteyne my L. Chiefe Justice of the K. Benche and Sir Walter Mildmaye's assente, I wolde not doubte to have the assente also of the whole parishe, that ye leade might goe to the coveringe of Powles.... Now remayneth only this scruple—How shall the parisshe be providett of a churche? That is thus answered: There is an house adjoininge, wch was the *Fratrie*, as they termed it, a very fayre and a large house, and indeed al-readye: if it were purged, it lacketh nothinge but the name of a churche; is well buylded of free stone, garnished inwarde aboute with marble pyllers, large windowes, etc. I assure you, without partialitie, if it were roofed up, it were farre more beautiful and conveniente than the other. Yt is provided with goode sclate. If we mighte have the leade, we wolde compownde with my L. Rich for convertinge the said *Fratrie* to a *Churche*, and wee wylle also supplye all imperfections of the same, and not desire the p'isshe to remove tylle the other be meete and conveniente to goe to. [13]

17 Lord Rich thought favourably of the proposal; but that fears were entertained elsewhere would seem probable from a second letter, in which Grindal writes as follows:

For S. Bartholomewes—I meane not to pulle it downe, but to change it for a Churche more conveniente ... unlesse some strange opinion shulde arise that prayer were more acceptable under leade than under sclate.

18 The long period of neglect and desecration which follows is rather to be inferred from the condition of the buildings in the early part of the nineteenth century than from any actual records respecting them. What that condition was in 1809 is described in two letters which appeared in "The Gentleman's Magazine" for March and April in that year. They were written in a spirit of indignation at the behaviour of "a powerful junto" which had been formed in the parish to sweep the whole structure away, church included, on the pretext that part of the choir was in danger of tumbling down. It had, however, been saved by the exertions and judicious repairs of

Mr. Hardwick, to whom the writer pays a just compliment for his timely action against the particular committee. He then goes on with a lamentable picture of what met his eyes on a "recent survey" of the Priory, which he had previously examined in 1791, when it was pretty much in the same state. [14] The Lady Chapel was still in existence, but wholly filled up with modern tenements; the north transept was more or less destroyed, and the arch bricked up to reduce that side of the church to a level, while the south transept—a ruin without a roof—was walled off from the church, and used as a burial-ground. The eastern side of the cloister was all that remained of the quadrangle, and was turned to account as a "comfortable eight-stall stable" for horses. The site of the north cloister was occupied by a blacksmith's forge, a public house, and certain private offices; the south and west being covered with store-rooms and coach-houses. Of the Chapter House the remaining walls were "no higher than a dado," and under them the timber was stored after treatment in the sawpit of the enclosure. The dormitory to the south of the Chapter House had been demolished, and the crypt beneath it bricked off into divisions for stores, with a common thoroughfare open between them. It may here be mentioned that a close examination of the ground has shown that there was formerly the usual "slype," or open pathway, running from the cloister-garth, between the south transept and the Chapter House, to the canons' cemetery on the southern side of the Lady Chapel.

The building against the south wall of the choir (probably the sacristy, though called a chapel) is described as a magnificent structure, of about the time of Edward III, with windows on the eastern and southern sides, and a grand arch (then latticed up) which formerly connected it with the south transept. It was being used as a store-room for hops. The chapel to the east of this was destroyed in its upper part, and the windows had lost their arched heads, though the columns and architraves to the jambs remained, showing some very delicate and beautiful work, which was also remarkably fine in the dado mouldings. The ceiling of the church—the wreck of the Tudor open-worked timber roof—had been "pared down to a common pediment covering," supported on the heads of cherubim as corbels. The Doric altar-piece is contemptuously referred to as "a painted theatrical scene of architecture." [15]

19 While the subordinate buildings were dropping into ruin, the church, besides having suffered from fire and neglect, had been disfigured by a long series of repairs and embellishments, the character of which may be inferred from the glaring instances pointed out in the letters just quoted. The other alterations made in the interior may be briefly summarized as follows: The level of the floor was raised by a thick deposit of earth; the walls were enveloped in whitewash, to the concealment of the ancient mural paintings and certain delicate sculptured ornament; and high pews were erected, which reached almost to the capitals of the piers. The openings of the triforium were bricked up—in some cases entirely obliterated—and at the east end, above the altar-piece just mentioned, there rose a brick wall, pierced with two ugly round-headed windows, filled with square panes of glass, and destitute of mullions and tracery. The space between the termination thus formed and the original apse went by the name of "Purgatory," as a receptacle for human bones, some thousands of which were found to have accumulated when it was cleared out in 1836. [16]

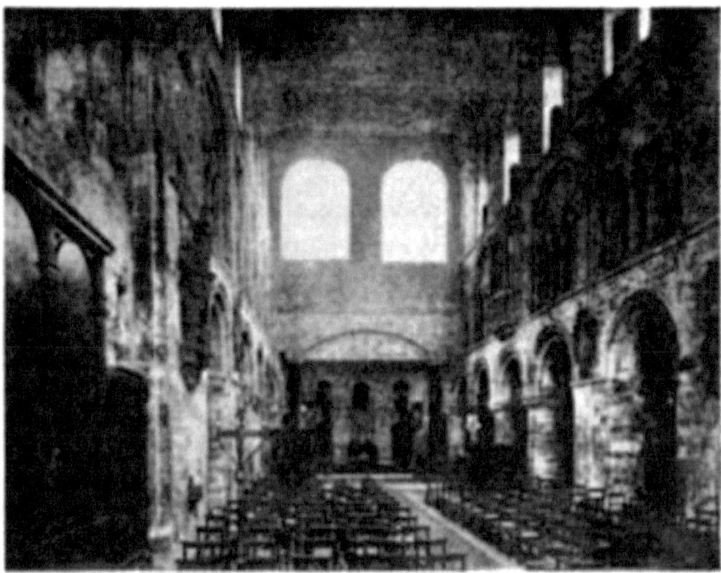

THE CHOIR BEFORE RESTORATION, SHOWING THE FACTORY

FLOOR EXTENDING OVER THE APSE AND SUPPORTED BY
TWO IRON COLUMNS

20 The secularization of this extreme eastern part of the church is
traced to the first purchaser from the Government, who held that
the sanctuary was bounded by the straight wall which there ran
across it. A more modern consequence than that just mentioned was
the intrusion into the triforium of a Nonconformist school, which
was held there during the eighteenth century, in connection with a
chapel belonging to the particular denomination immediately outside, having a convenient access to the triforium from its own gal-
leries. Another encroachment was a fringe manufactory, which
extended westwards along the triforium so as to include Prior Bolton's window, and held its ground for some time after the main
arcading of the apse had been restored. Visitors to the church before
the restoration was complete will remember a substantial iron bar
which was carried across the curve, above the altar, to strengthen
the walls—an eyesore which could not be removed till the intruding
factory was bought out (*vide infra*).

The real work of restoration was begun in 1863 by the late Rev.
John Abbiss, then Rector of the parish, who raised something like
£5,000, and spent it in reducing the floor to its original level, removing the pews (which had previously been lowered), repairing the
walls and piers, and rebuilding the central part of the apse, which
had been pulled down early in the fifteenth century, as already
explained.

21 Outside the church a dry area was formed for the better pro-
tection of the fabric against the subsidence known to follow on the
ignorance, or indifference, of early builders as to underlying strata.
All this was accomplished in three years, when the money was ex-
hausted, and a fresh fund had to be created for the continuation of
the restorative work. In raising subscriptions the then patron of the
living, the Rev. F. P. Phillips, was well supported by the parishion-
ers, the City Companies, the Charity Commissioners (out of the City
Ecclesiastical Funds), and the general public, with the result that a
sum of over £28,000 was got together. The chief individual contribu-
tor was the patron himself, who purchased the projecting fringe
factory for £6,500, [17] and completed the restoration of the apse at

his own expense. At the same time the church was provided with a new roof, and the blacksmith's forge, which occupied the site of the north transept, was bought out. On the 30th November, 1886, the restored portions were formally opened, the actual work having started about two years before, under the active interest of the Rev. William Panckridge, who succeeded Mr. Abbiss in the Rectory.

The long list of works undertaken and completed from 1887 to 1893, under the succeeding Rector, the Rev. Sir J. Borradaile Savory, Bart., includes the restoration of both transepts, the opening out of both sides of the choir triforium, [18] the erection of the north and west porches, the refacing of the west front, the reparation of the brick tower, and the re-hanging of the bells, besides numerous external and internal details.

The crowning work was the reconstruction of the Lady Chapel, which was not completed till 1896, after the tedious business of releasing it from its secular holders, and the recovery of the original design amidst the mutilation in which they left it. The whole has been admirably carried through by Sir Aston Webb, R.A., who has restored the precious fabric as nearly as possible to its original state, by replacing what was destroyed, and revealing what was concealed when the difficult task was committed to him.

22 The restoration has since been extended to three bays on the eastern side of the cloister, all that remained of the original quadrangle, and these in a sadly ruinous state. Whether the cloisters were completed by Rahere is a matter of conjecture; but it may be fairly assumed that they were begun by him as a necessary part of the monastery. The surviving Norman fragments point to the twelfth century as the date of their first erection. It is certain that they were rebuilt in the fifteenth, for besides the architectural remains of that period, there is historical evidence that the work was done under Prior John Watford soon after his appointment in 1404. For in September, 1409, Pope Alexander V, when making a grant of Indulgences to those who visited and gave alms at the church on Maundy Thursday, Good Friday, Holy Saturday, and the Feast of the Assumption, expressly mentions the reconstruction of the Cloisters and Chapter House by the Prior among the reasons which had induced him to confer the privilege.

When the monastery was suppressed, the archway leading into the east cloister from the church was built up, and the doors were taken from it—in all probability to be transferred (in 1544) to the principal entrance at the western end of the truncated building.

In the reconstruction attempted by the Dominican Friars, it seems that, instead of re-opening the cloister-arch to its full extent, they contented themselves with inserting a smaller doorway within it, the jambs and lintel of which were discovered in the rubble masonry when the arch was opened out in 1905. On the suppression of the Dominicans by Queen Elizabeth, the cloisters passed again into secular hands, and disappear from history until the year 1742, when there is a record of the stabling that occupied the ruins till our own day, with the temporary interruption of a fire in 1830, which brought most of the eastern side to the ground. The stables were afterwards rebuilt, and left undisturbed till 1900, when negotiations were opened for the purchase of the freehold from the owners.

23 It was not till Michaelmas, 1904, that possession, even of a part, could be obtained, as there were various leasehold interests to be reckoned with, and many beneficiaries to be satisfied, whose rights will not be finally extinguished until June, 1926. But excavation was at once commenced, and the actual rebuilding in 1905. It need hardly be said that all that has been discovered of the ancient work, here and elsewhere, whether above or below ground, has been carefully preserved, and incorporated (as far as possible *in situ*) into the restoration.

Footnotes

[1] I. "Liber fundationis ecclesiae et prioratus S. Bartholomaei in West-Smithfield, London; per Raherum qui illic religiosos viros secundum regulam S. patris Augustini aggregavit, iisdemque per XXII annos prioris dignitate et officio functus praetuit, et de miraculis ipsius."

II. "Idem liber Anglice."

Both are on parchment, in pages of the same (quarto) size, and bound together in a single volume of eighty-three leaves, divided almost equally between the Latin and English versions.—Cottonian MSS. Vespasian, B. ix.

[2] "When he attained the flower of youth, he began to haunt the households of noblemen and the palaces of princes, where, under every elbow of them, he spread their cushions, with apings and flatterings delectably anointing their eyes, to draw to him their friendships. And yet he was not content with this, but haunted the King's palace, and among the noisefull press of that tumultuous Court enforced himself with jollity and carnal suavity, by the which he might draw to him the hearts of many a one."—Cottonian MS., *ut supra*.

[3] Cottonian MS.

[4] *Ibid.*

[5] This Richard de Belmeis (Beauvais) was the first of two bishops of the same name, and held the See of London for twenty years (1108-1128).

The name of Rahere, which appears in various forms, suggests a French origin; and from the fact that it occurs in the signature, or attestation, of certain documents discovered in Brittany, as well as from the close relations between the bishop and the founder of St. Bartholomew's, it is conjectured that they both came from the same neighbourhood. Otherwise their joint interest in the foundation at Smithfield is sufficiently accounted for by the benevolent object and the situation within the London diocese.

Leland gives the credit of the foundation to Henry I, as having granted the land out of the royal domain.

[6] The Canons Regular of St. Augustine (of Hippo) are said to have been founded at Avignon in or about 1061. Their first establishment in England was at Colchester (*circa* 1105), where the picturesque ruins of the Priory Church, dedicated to St. Botolph, are all that remain of the monastic buildings. The habit consisted of a black cassock with a white rochet, over which a black cloak and hood were worn, thus leading to their familiar name of the Black Canons—not to be confused with the Black *Friars*, a Dominican Order of mendicants, introduced at St. Bartholomew's Priory under Queen Mary. From an anecdote related by Matthew Paris (under the year 1250), and quoted in most accounts of the Priory, it seems that the inmates, while recognizing the authority of the Bishop of London,

were extremely jealous of outside interference. The Archbishop of Canterbury (Boniface of Savoy) had ventured to include St. Bartholomew's in one of his visitations. He was received with becoming dignity by the sub-prior, but politely warned against going beyond his jurisdiction. This so enraged his Grace that he struck the sub-prior in the face, and, "with many oaths," rent in pieces the rich cope he was wearing, treading it under his feet, and thrusting the sub-prior against a pillar of the chancel with such violence as almost to kill him. A general conflict followed between the Canons and the Archbishop's attendants, which was taken up outside and set the whole city in an uproar.

[7] *Vide* Dr. Norman Moore's edition from the copy in the Record Office.

[8] There had been a decline in public interest for some years before 1691, when the abuses which had grown round the celebration led to its reduction from fourteen to four days: but the fair lingered on in a degenerate state till it was last proclaimed by the Lord Mayor in 1850, and finally ceased in 1855. The live cattle market, so vividly described, with its attendant nuisances, in the twenty-first chapter of "Oliver Twist," was closed at the same time, and the business transferred to the new Caledonian Market. The open pens at Smithfield have been superseded by covered buildings, to which the old Newgate Market has been removed, and considerably developed, for the sale of meat, the slaughtering for the most part being done locally in the various places whence the supplies are derived.

The memory of old associations is preserved in the street which runs along the north side of the church, and still bears the name of "Cloth Fair": and the site of "Pye Corner," where the great fire of 1666 reached its limit, is marked by a tablet in the wall, at the entrance to Cock Lane in Giltspur Street, a short distance to the southwest. The place took its name from the "Court of Pie-Powder," which was held during the fair here, as at similar gatherings throughout the country, to deal expeditiously with disturbers of the peace. The etymology is traced to the old French *pied pouldré*, with supposed reference to the dusty feet of pedlars and others who came before the court—now extinguished in the more modern Petty Sessions.

A lively description of the fair, in its palmy days, is given in a tract, printed in 1641 for Richard Harper at the "Bible and Harp" in Smithfield, entitled, "Bartholomew Fair, or varieties of fancies, where you may find a faire of wares, and all to please your mind, with the several enormityes and misdemeanours which are there seen and heard."

Among the more gloomy associations of Smithfield are the martyrdoms which took place there during the Marian persecution of 1555-57. Of the victims, John Rogers, John Bradford, and John Philpot are commemorated in a modern tablet let into the wall of the hospital facing the square where they suffered. The church to their memory, referred to in the inscription, is in St. John Street Road, where it was built as a Chapel-of-Ease to the parish church of St. John-of-Jerusalem, founded by the Knights Hospitallers in 1185.

[9] The late Mr. J. H. Parker was inclined to think there was a tower in each corner (though two only could be represented in the seal), as was not unusual in France and elsewhere, but rarely the case in England. (See his lecture delivered in the church on 13th July, 1863.)

[10] *Vide* "Henry VIII and the English Monasteries," by the Rt. Rev. Abbot Gasquet, D.D., O.S.B., for an able statement of the case for the communities: and an article by G. G. Perry ("Eng. Hist. Review," April, 1889), on "Episcopal Visitations of the Austin Canons," for some cases of laxity.

[11] The Dominicans were introduced at St. Bartholomew's in 1556, when their old monastery (dating from 1276), near the north end of Blackfriars Bridge, was no longer available. Possibly their work and reputation in making converts may have had some influence on the choice of the Order, which, moreover, was governed by the Augustinian rule, adopted (with additions) by their founder in 1215, and so far brought the community under the traditions of their predecessors. The members at Smithfield consisted of English, Spanish, and Belgian friars, and Fr. William Perrin, O.P., was appointed as their chief. When he died in 1558, Fr. Richard Hargrave was elected in his place, but was not allowed to take office, appar-

ently in view of the suppression which was impending when the Letters Patent from the General, confirming his election, reached England in the following year. By the time of the actual expulsion (13th July, 1559) the community had been reduced by deaths and migrations to "three priests and one young man," who would seem to have conformed, in preference to leaving the country. (*Vide* "The Elizabethan Religious Settlement," ch. iv, by Dom H. N. Birt, O.S.B.)

For the general history of the Black Friars the reader is referred to Archbishop Alemany's "Life of St. Dominic, with a Sketch of the Dominican Order," the "Etudes sur l'Ordre de St. Dominique" by D'Anzas, and "The Coming of the Friars" by Dr. Aug. Jessopp. The "Chronica Majora" of Matthew Paris afford some lively reading on the subject.

[12] It is possible that investigations now pending may involve a slight rearrangement of this conjectural plan, as those previously drawn have similarly been modified from time to time by fresh discoveries.

[13] This suggestion of Bishop Grindal's recalls the case of Beaulieu Abbey where the beautiful refectory is still preserved as the parish church.

[14] The church had been "restored" in 1789 by Mr. George Dance, architect to the hospital, in a spirit which may be inferred from the description of the interior given above. A more sympathetic restoration was inaugurated by Mr. Philip Hardwick in 1823.

[15] When the church was repaired by Mr. John Blyth in 1836, this painting was removed, and a range of columns, bearing small semicircular arches, substituted for it as a reredos. During these alterations it was discovered that the stone wall (erected by de Walden) between the wooden altar-piece and the original apse, was painted in bright red tempera, sprinkled with black stars.

The above-mentioned letters are attributed to Mr. John Carter, but are merely signed by "An Architect."

[16] It would probably be unfair to infer any unusual neglect in spiritual matters from the architectural conditions. In Paterson's "Pietas Londinensis" there is a list of public services at many London churches, as held in the early part of the eighteenth century.

The services at St. Bartholomew-the-Great are there quoted as "Daily in the last week in the month at 11 a.m. and 5 p.m.," and at St. Bartholomew-the-Less as "Daily at 11 a.m."

[17] It should be stated that the fringe factory had covered the remains of the crypt and Lady Chapel, besides projecting some twenty feet into the east end of the church. The architects for these earlier restorations were Professor Hayter Lewis and Mr. Slater, who deserve credit for their careful preservation of the old work.

[18] The obstruction on the south side of the triforium has been already mentioned. The northern side was used for the parochial boys' school for many years down to 1892, when the scholars were transferred to the new schools built for them adjoining the church.

24

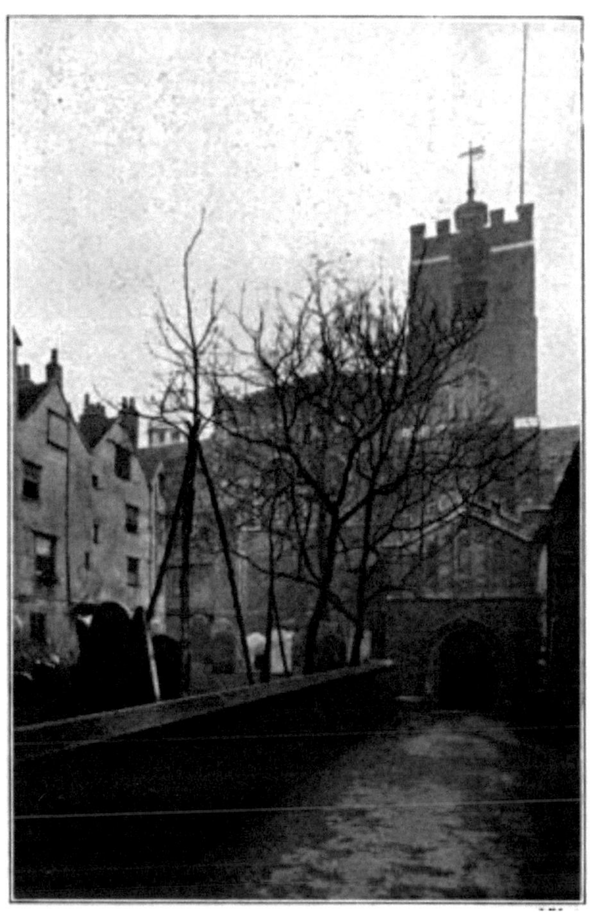

THE PRIORY CHURCH FROM THE WEST 25

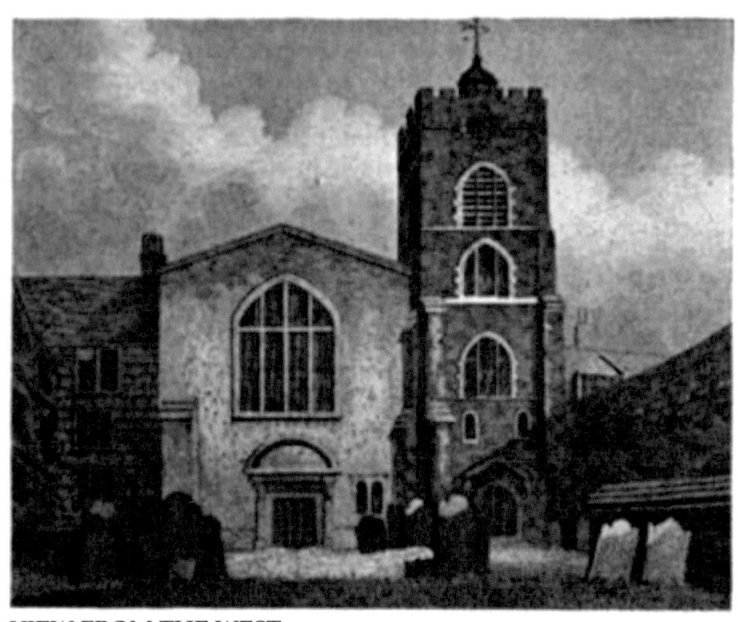

VIEW FROM THE WEST
From a print of 1810

CHAPTER II

THE EXTERIOR

The church lies in a general east and west direction, and, at the present day, consists of the Choir and encircling Ambulatory, Lady Chapel, north and south Transepts, with the lower stage of the central Tower, one bay of the ancient Nave, three bays of the Cloister, and a seventeenth-century brick Tower — the whole hidden behind the houses, in an obscure corner of West Smithfield, by no means easy for a stranger to discover. It will be well for him, therefore, in the first place, to make his way to the better known buildings of St. Bartholomew's Hospital, and then walk across the open square, between them and Smithfield Market, to its eastern side, where he will find the entrance close to the narrow street called Cloth Fair.

The Gateway is interesting, as a surviving fragment of the Early-English period, supposed by some authorities to mark the site of the original west front, of which they regard it as having formed part — the entrance to the south aisle — which was allowed to stand, after the grand central porch, and a corresponding doorway on the northern side, were destroyed with the nave. More probable is the conjecture that it was merely the entrance to the monastic enclosure, turned to account as a ready-made structure when the work at the church was the reverse of constructive, as it seems too large and too high for a mere doorway at the end of an aisle, besides being rather too far from the church to agree with its supposed dimensions. The modern iron gate is surmounted by a gilded cross and the name of the church on a framework in the tympanum. The arch is acutely pointed, and moulded in four orders, with a tooth ornament in the hollows, and is in tolerably good condition; but the supporting shafts have been superseded by a wall on each side, with the circular moulded capitals (much decayed) above it, the bases either being destroyed or buried in the earth beneath. The gateway is in a line with the houses facing the public square, which touch it on both sides, and are carried on without interruption above the opening.

When the floor of the church was lowered to its original level in 1863-6, the present approach to it was made by an excavation through the churchyard, which covered the site of the nave, and is now walled off on the northern side of the passage.

The gravestones are of comparatively modern date, and of no special interest. A few of them have been left against the wall on the right, where there is something of more antiquarian value in a collection of *débris* from the old building, containing the bases of some of the Early-English columns in their original place, but hopelessly mutilated.

27 The existing **West Front** dates from the time when the nave was destroyed. In 1893 a great improvement was made in its appearance by refacing the wall with flint and stone, and otherwise ornamenting the surface, to bring it into uniformity with the porch which was then built at that end of the church. There are now three round-headed recesses in the central portion of the wall, those at the extremities containing narrow windows; a band of chequered stonework is carried across the space beneath them, and a small circular window inserted above. It may be mentioned here that the pointed arch has generally been adopted in the new work, to distinguish it from the old, but the characteristic massiveness and predominant scale of the original has been preserved throughout the restoration. A practical illustration of these principles will be seen in **The Porch**, as an ingenious compromise between the older and newer types of architecture which are brought together in the main fabric. It is built of a combination of flint and Portland stone, like the wall-front just described, with which it is connected by a small circular tower and an oblong extension on the northern side. The two storeys of which it consists are divided externally by a band of chequered diaper. The shallow arch of the doorway is simply moulded and very slightly pointed, suggesting a transition from the Romanesque to the Early-English style, while the Perpendicular is represented in the battlements on the roof and the octagonal turret on the southern side. In a niche above the apex of the arch, and on a bracket displaying the Priory arms, upheld by two angels, stands a figure of Rahere, the founder, with his left hand raised in benediction, and in his right a model of the church. The design of this little edifice is taken from one of the ancient seals (see Illustration 9 in the Appendix), and shows the central tower, with a round turret at each end, and a small building (probably the original Lady Chapel) pro-

jecting from the east. Rahere's features are copied from the effigy on his tomb, which is believed to be an authentic portrait. The figure occupies the central position in the higher storey, with three arched recesses on either side (the middle one in each case containing a window), diminishing in height outwards, in harmony with the lines of the roof. The ceiling within the porch is groined in four divisions; and the "priest's chamber" above it makes a convenient private room for the rector of the parish. This new porch bears its own date (1893), and the date of the foundation, seven hundred and seventy years earlier. [1]

28 **The Brick Tower**, built in 1628, is said to have been altered to some extent in subsequent repairs, which have not improved its appearance. So at least say the admirers of King Charles I, who argue that nothing quite so hideous could have been erected in his reign. It is a plain square structure, seventy-five feet in height, in four stages, gradually diminishing in area upwards, the lower part supported by buttresses, and the summit crowned by battlements, with a small bell-turret and vane. More interesting than the tower itself—which is, in fact, an incongruous addition to the church—are the **Bells** which it contains, a precious inheritance from the Augustinian Canons, and in some respects the most remarkable in London. The foundry stamp shows them to have been cast by Thomas Bullisdon, who died about 1510. They are the smaller five of a ring of twelve, six of which were sold at the Dissolution to the Church of St. Sepulchre, Holborn, where they have since been re-cast, and one has disappeared from history.

The measurements and inscriptions are as follows:

1. Sancte Bartholemeo: Ora pro nobis. Diameter 22 in.

2. Sancta Katerina: Ora pro nobis. Diameter 24 in.

3. Sancta Anna: Ora pro nobis. Diameter 26¾ in.

4. Sancte Johannes Baptiste: Ora pro nobis. Diameter 29¼ in.

5. Sancte Petre: Ora pro nobis. Diameter 31 in.

The clock-bell, in the cage on the top, is inscribed, "T. Mears of London Fecit 1814." Diameter about 25 inches.

29 The churchyard is overlooked on its northern side by the back windows of some rickety old wooden houses, suggestive of an easy conflagration, and dangerously near the church. They date from the time of Queen Elizabeth, and stand on a piece of the ground formerly devoted to Bartholomew Fair, the memory of which is perpetuated in the adjoining street (Cloth Fair), where the humble shops in front of the same houses are said to be a survival of the ancient booths. They run close up to the **North Porch**, which projects into the street from the transept. It was erected in 1893, at the same time that the transept was restored. The porch is similar in material and character to that on the west, with some differences in detail, the chief of which are that the figure over the door represents St. Bartholomew, with only one window on each side of it—in this case square-headed, with a label-moulding—and the chequered diaper covers the whole wall-surface of the upper storey. The Saint is raising his right hand in the act of blessing, and holds in the left a knife, which has become his emblem, as the instrument of his passion. A scroll entwined about the effigy bears the appropriate words (in English) from Rahere's vision: *Almighty God this spiritual house shall inhabit and hallow it.* The upper chamber here is reserved for the mission-lady working in the district.

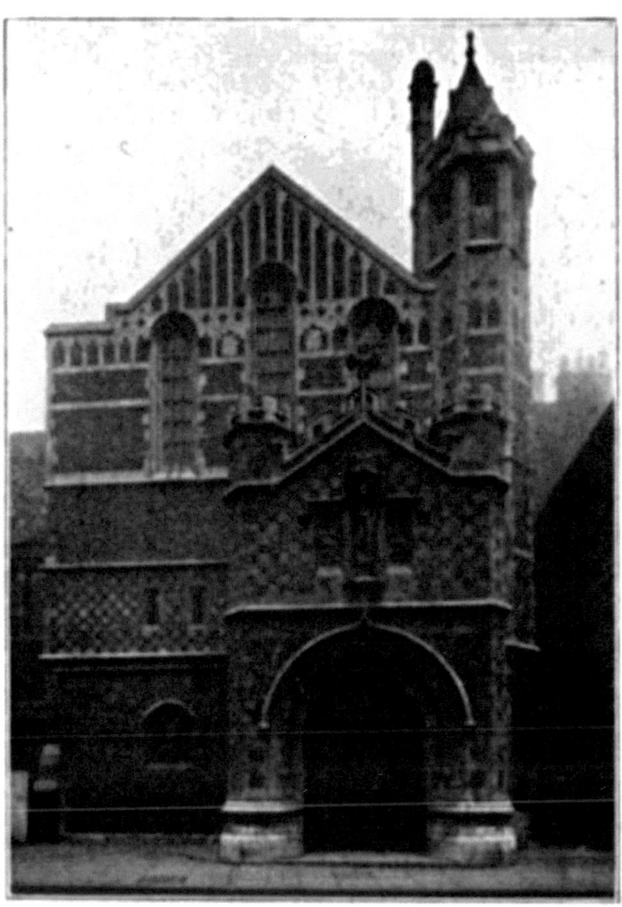

THE NORTH PORCH

30 The face of the transept visible above displays three lancet-headed windows of the clerestory; the spaces are laid out in ornamental panels; and there is an octagonal turret on the right, with battlements and a pointed roof.

The rest of the church is hemmed in, and for the most part concealed, by tumble-down houses, forming a labyrinth of narrow winding passages about the walls, and even encroaching upon them — a bit of old London which has escaped the modern spirit of improvement, and would appear to be full of suggestive material for the writer of romance. As we thread our way through this network round the east end and south side, to reach the entrance once more, we get an occasional glimpse of the choir and Lady Chapel through a gap in the surrounding buildings; but are far more impressed with the sense of poverty and ruin than by anything in the way of architecture, which can be much better seen and described from within. The new schools in the south-east corner (built to supersede the old structure which still remains attached to the north triforium) are worth a visit *en route*: and so, perhaps, is the abandoned burial-ground outside the south transept, if only as a melancholy souvenir of the past.

The church is open every day, and the services are as follows:

Sundays

8.15 a.m.	Holy Communion.
11 a.m.	Mattins.
11.45 a.m.	Holy Communion (choral) and Sermon.
4 p.m.	Children's Service and Catechizing.
7 p.m.	Evensong and Sermon.

Saints' Days

8.15 a.m.	Holy Communion.
11 a.m.	Mattins.
8.30 p.m.	Evensong and Sermon.

Ordinary Days

11 a.m.	Mattins.
4 p.m.	Evensong, except on Wednesdays, when the arrangement is the same as for Saints' Days.

31

FOOTNOTE

[1] Within the porch a tablet on the south wall gives a list of the Priors and Rectors. On the opposite wall another tablet, recording some of the restorative work, forms part of the memorial to Sir Borradaile Savory. For the rest of the memorial see notes on pp. 48 and 57.

32

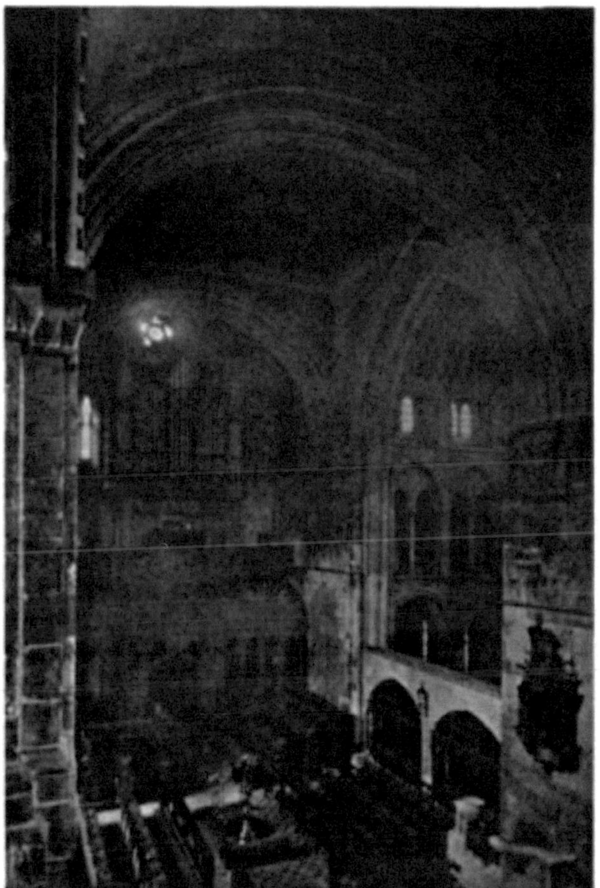

VIEW OF THE CROSSING FROM THE TRIFORIUM

Table of
Contents
33

CHAPTER III

THE INTERIOR

As soon as the visitor enters the church, he will be able to contrast the Norman work of the twelfth century with that which succeeded it in the thirteenth, as both are brought into juxtaposition immediately within the western doorway. The surviving **Bay of the Nave**, which probably marks the boundary of the monastic choir, now answers the purpose of a vestibule to the church, from the body of which it is separated by the organ-screen, the instrument being carried on a gallery built against the western wall. The nave arches, at each end of the passage thus formed, are semicircular in shape, with a zigzag moulding on the inner sides, and rest on massive rounded piers, with square bases and abaci and simple cushioned capitals—the whole obviously of early twelfth century date. The northern arch has been built up, and a small Tudor doorway, inserted in the wall, gives access to the transept.

At right angles with the southern arch, and on each side of the entrance to the choir aisle, or ambulatory, there is a cluster of **Early English Columns**, still bearing a portion of the vaulting-shafts, from which it can be seen that the pitch of the roof to the nave aisle was much higher than that of the ambulatory to which it was attached, probably implying a corresponding difference in the height of the nave. The slender columns on both sides are alike in their moulded bases, which resemble those left (*in situ*) among the ruins outside, as far as the latter can be discerned; but there is an interesting variety in other details, the capitals of the northern group being cut into foliage, while they are moulded on the south, where also the shafts are banded.

34 **The Organ-screen** (modern) is an elegant piece of work in oak, panelled and canopied in the Perpendicular style. With the organ-front above, it forms an admirable background to the choir-stalls, which are arranged in the space within the old central tower, the seats for the congregation being carried along towards the east, facing each other chapel-wise, in continuation of the stalls on either side. A description of the organ will be found in the Appendix.

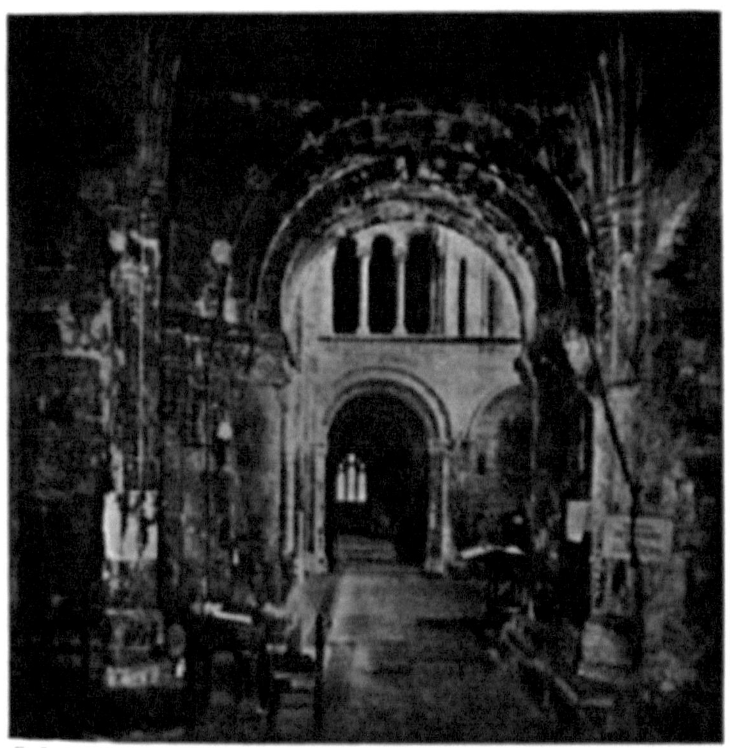

THE SOUTH AISLE FROM THE WEST, SHOWING THE EARLY
ENGLISH SHAFTS

35 **The Tower Arches** are worth particular notice. Those on the
north and south are pointed, and much narrower than the others,
which have a bold semicircular sweep. An intelligible reason sometimes assigned for the difference is that the area enclosed is not
exactly square, and that it became necessary for the builders to carry
the transept-arches to a point, to accommodate them to the oblong
plan, and bring the upper mouldings into line with those of the
rounded arches between the choir and nave. On this supposition the
result has been called "an incidental use of the pointed arch," examples of which occur elsewhere (*e.g.*, at Christ Church, Oxford, and
other churches of the transitional period) before it became a distin-
guishing feature of the later style. It is tolerably certain, however,
that the tower was rebuilt in the fifteenth century, and that the

48

north and south arches were then altered from their first design. And their appearance is strongly in favour of a reconstruction; for it will be noticed that, instead of the usual elegant inclination in a continuous curve from the spring to the apex, they rise perpendicularly for some distance above the piers on either side, and then take rather an abrupt turn inwards, suggesting the imposition of a pointed heading on an original stilted form. Further signs of alteration appear on the northern side, where the capitals have been recut in the Perpendicular fashion; but the Norman pilasters and mouldings on the south remain untouched. On both sides the double serrated line of moulding claims attention, as an example of the "saw-tooth" ornament found in early work. A difference will be observed in the corbels supporting the mouldings of the eastern and western arches. The former are much more boldly cut, with all the appearance of original work, while those on the west would seem to have been modified by some architect of the Perpendicular age. In the decoration of the inner tower walls there is a lozenge-shaped panel in each of the spandrels, sculptured into a floral ornament something like the Greek honeysuckle, a shallow arcading in the angles, and a cornice of zigzag moulding extending round the walls, immediately below the modern ceiling (1886) of panelled oak.

36 The piers at the angles of the tower are not very much more massive than the adjacent walls, and do not strike one as capable of sustaining a superstructure of any great weight. It may therefore be inferred that the tower was a low one, as is in fact borne out by the representation on the Priory seal, where the circular turrets at each end of the church are shown to exceed it in height. **The North Transept**, which had been occupied for many years as a blacksmith's forge, was re-opened on 5th June, 1893, after restoration to something like its original state. It is now used as a morning chapel, with an altar in a recess on the north side, slightly to the east of the porch already described, by which the church is entered from Cloth Fair. [1]

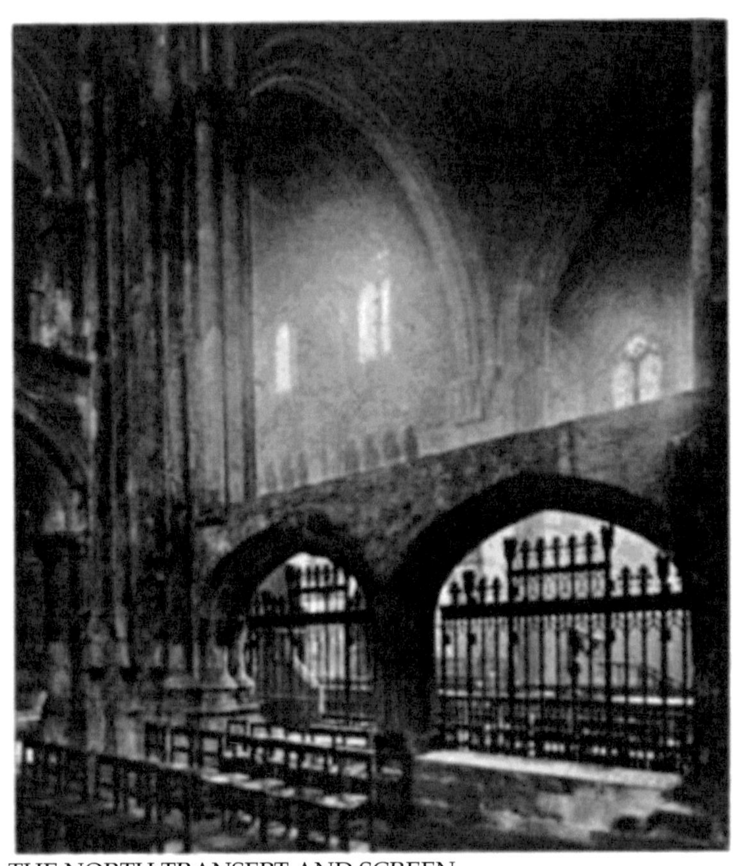

THE NORTH TRANSEPT AND SCREEN
37

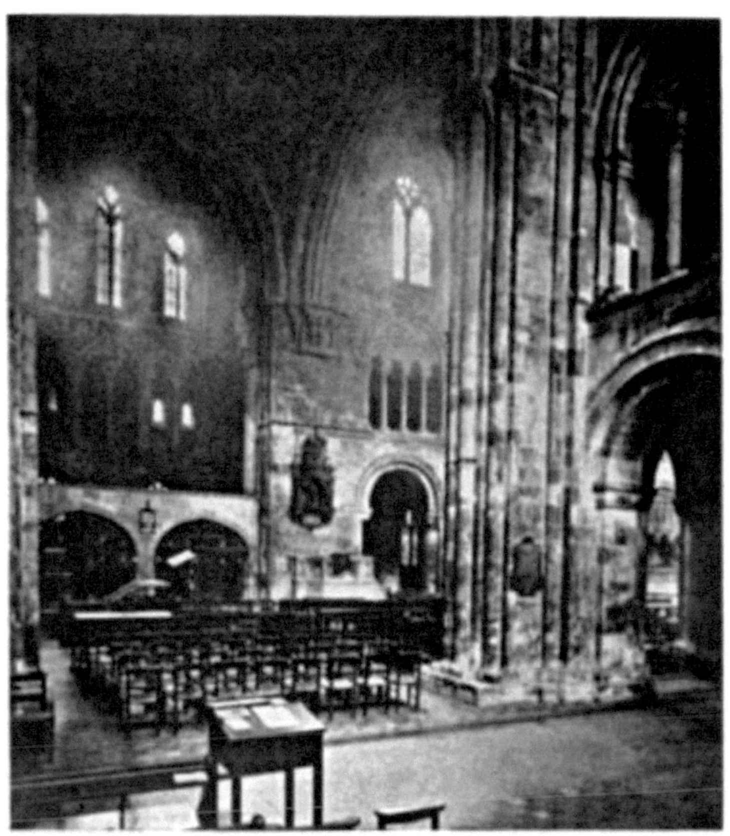

THE NORTH TRANSEPT FROM THE SOUTH

38 Both transepts had been injured by fire, and were originally much deeper than they are at present, but to have rebuilt them exactly on the old lines would have involved the suppression of a right of way and the purchase of neighbouring properties, besides adding to the cost of heating and maintenance, expenses which the funds would not allow. Here, as elsewhere, the old work, as far as it remained, has been left undisturbed, and simply incorporated into the new, the architect contenting himself with removing the modern walls which had been set up at the extremities to keep out the weather, providing abutments to strengthen the central arches, and supplying what was wanted to complete the first design within the

more limited area. During the reconstruction of this transept the fine arcaded **Stone Screen** was revealed which separates it from the space within the tower. The screen was buried some four feet in earth, and the upper part entirely concealed by the smithy. The style shows it to be of the fifteenth century, when there was probably a similar screen on the opposite side of the choir, the two backing the stalls, which are known to have been carried under the tower. The existing screen is divided into two wide arches, slightly depressed, with a moulding in four orders. It has been refaced on the choir side, and a partition of ironwork, ornamented with coloured coats of arms, inserted in the open spaces, to serve as a barrier without obstructing the view in either direction.

Under one of the arches there is a stone coffin, with a much decayed cover of Purbeck marble, which is supposed to have contained the body of a Prior. It was opened for examination during the rebuilding, when a skeleton was found within it, with sandals still on the feet, but as the skull was gone it was evident that the coffin had previously been opened. In the arch by its side there was another coffin of the same character, which has unfortunately been shifted to the north ambulatory. It is without a cover, and the skeleton is no longer there; but the leaden envelope remains, more or less in the state in which it was folded round the corpse. The arched recess on the east, by the side of the opening to the ambulatory, is supposed to have been the entrance to the Walden Chantry; but it has been built up with a return-wall.

The triforium is continuous through all three walls of the transept, each bay consisting of a double pointed arch, except that above the ambulatory, where the surviving Norman fragment shows three round-headed openings, included in a semicircular arch with billet moulding. The clerestory in the north wall, where the work is entirely new, is ornamented with a traceried arcading on an interior plane, which has a very beautiful effect.

39 **The South Transept**, opened after restoration on 14th March, 1891, had been turned to account as a burial-ground, supplementary to that at the west end. The side walls were allowed to stand for the enclosure, but the south wall was pulled down, and another erected within the space, to separate the "Green Churchyard," as it

was called, from the church. In this case, therefore, the restoration meant little more than the removal of the intercepting wall to open out the transept, and building a new one at the extremity, with a partial reconstruction of those which were decayed to connect them with it. In the renovation of both transepts blue Bath stone has been used internally, and Portland stone with flints for the exterior. The conservative nature of the work is here seen in the side walls, each of which retains a bay of the old Norman triforium, with its round-headed divisions, to which a new bay has been added, with a slightly pointed arcade, as a connection, without any violent contrast, between the older parts of the transept and the new south wall. This presents an agreeable variety to that facing it in the opposite transept. In the upper stage, instead of a triforium and clerestory, there are three tall windows of two lights each, the central being carried above the others, and distinguished by a more ornate tracery, here taking a cruciform pattern above the trefoil-headed divisions, instead of a foliated circle as in the side windows. The arcading in which they are all placed is severely simple in character, the slightly pointed headings resting on plain shafts, with moulded bases and capitals—the whole composition a pleasing relief to the heavier architecture on each side without being discordant. The same may be said of the lower stage, also arcaded in three divisions, corresponding with those above, but rather more massive in character. The central arch forms a porch, giving access to the church on that side, with a recess to the east and west of it, each lighted by a dwarfed window. The eastern of these recesses answers the purpose of a baptistery. **The Font** dates from the early fifteenth century, and is octagonal in shape, with a tall cover, crocketed at the angles, suspended on a swivel above it. The facets of the octagon are perfectly plain, but there is an oblong incision in one of them which looks very much like the matrix of a brass, or the seat of a sculptured panel, which has been removed. There is a traditional interest attaching to the font as that in which William Hogarth, the famous painter and satirist, was baptized. He was born in Bartholomew Close on 10th November, 1697, and his baptism is entered in the parish register on the 28th of 40 the same month. [2] It is recorded that the font had a narrow escape in the eighteenth century, when the Vestry ordered it to be removed for a new one, but fortunately the order was never carried out.

In a recess on the eastern side of the transept there is a monument to **Elizabeth Freshwater**, whose effigy, in the costume and ruff collar of her time, is shown kneeling at a small *priedieu*, with English and Latin inscriptions beneath:

Here lyeth interred the body of Elizabeth Freshwater, late wife of Thomas Freshwater, of Henbridge, in the County of Essex, Esquire; eldest daughter of John Orme of this parish, Gentleman, and Mary his wife. She died the 16th day of May Anno Domini 1617, being of the age of 26 years.

> Ut sic trina uno vulnere praeda cadat?
> Unam saeva feris; sed et uno hoc occidit ictu
> Uxor dulcis, amans filia, chara soror.

> (= O hasty death, how hast them so contrived
> Thy darts with venomous poison to direct
> That, by one cruel stroke, not one but three are killed,
> Sweet wife, a loving daughter, sister dear!)

The doorway beneath the monument opens on the staircase to the south triforium.

41 **The Choir**, now restored as nearly as possible to its original state, consists of five bays on each side, with an apsidal termination of five arches, distinguished from the others (mainly semicircular) by their "stilted" form and much narrower span, which, in fact, measures no more than the diameter of the intervening columns, and gives an appearance of extra massiveness to the east end of the church. All the arches display some approximation to the "horseshoe," in a slight inward inclination on either side towards the capitals on which they rest; but the shape is very definitely assumed in each of those immediately contiguous to the transverse curve. These are of the genuine "horseshoe" pattern characteristic of Arabian or Moorish buildings; and their exact similarity in detail, with their position facing one another at each extremity of the apse, would seem to indicate a structural necessity, or deliberate intention in the design, which, neither here nor elsewhere in the arcading, is to be

attributed to any subsidence, or imperfect workmanship, sometimes held to account for the deflection as a mere accident.

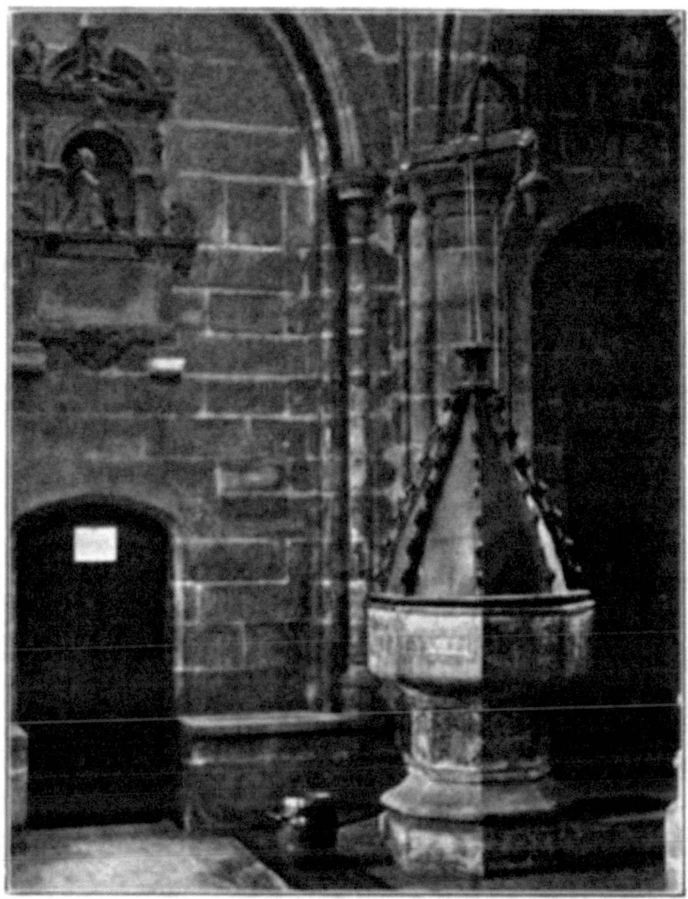

THE FONT AND THE FRESHWATER MONUMENT
42

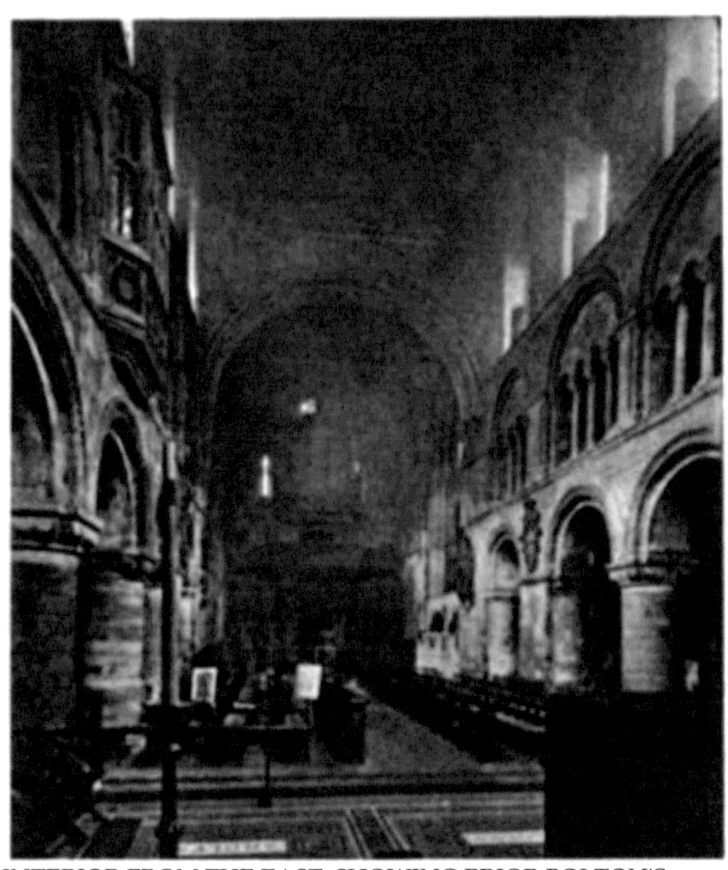

INTERIOR FROM THE EAST, SHOWING PRIOR BOLTON'S
GALLERY

43 The character of these arches, with the slightly domical vaults
noticeable in the adjacent aisles, has led some persons to detect an
Oriental influence in the building—possibly traceable to the visitors
from Byzantium whom the founder is said to have consulted while
it was in course of erection—though it is argued to the contrary that
these features are sufficiently accounted for by the general tendency
of Anglo-Norman architecture at the time, as illustrated elsewhere.

The arcading throughout rests on massive piers and circular columns, with square bases and abaci (incised at the angles) and low

cushioned capitals, ornamented with a simple scallop. Above the arches, on the choir side, there is a billet moulding, which is considered unique in that, instead of forming a separate decoration to each arch, it is carried along horizontally above the abaci on either side in a continuous line of ornament.

The Triforium consists of a series of rounded arches, the piers from which they spring being placed directly above those of the main arcade. Each of the side bays is divided into four compartments by small columns, above which the tympanum of the enclosing arch is occupied by a blank wall. The sequence is, of course, interrupted by the oriel window in the central bay on the south; and the narrower openings in the apse only admit of a twofold division. There are said to have been originally windows at the back of the triforium-gallery, as at Durham, Peterborough, and other Norman churches of the same period; but the mutilation and rebuilding in the external walls have greatly destroyed the original work.

44 **Prior Bolton's Window** was probably inserted about 1530, when the device of a "bolt in tun" was officially authorized for Bolton's arms, on his own choice, as presenting his name in the emblematical form then in vogue. The window is an "oriel" in the Perpendicular style, separated vertically by mullions into three lights in front, with one at each end of the projection, and horizontally by transoms into an upper and lower tier, the former having a trefoil heading to each division. There is a sloping hipped roof to the window, and a broad moulded corbel below it. The well-known rebus is boldly displayed upon the central of the five square panels (all sculptured) which adorn the face of this picturesque chamber (*oriolum*), probably built as a convenient private pew for the Prior, from which he could survey the whole of the choir and the Founder's tomb. The Tudor doorway, which now opens into the choir vestry at the eastern end of the south wall, has the Bolton rebus in the spandrels of the arch. [3]

The Clerestory.—In his reconstruction here Sir Aston Webb has followed the precedent of the Perpendicular work introduced in the fifteenth century, which, fortunately, had not been seriously injured in the upper part of the side walls. He has accordingly adopted that style in the apse, where the clerestory arcade is entirely new. It displays a series of five windows of two lights each, with traceried headings, and slender columns on the inner and outer plane, sufficient to uphold the arcading without intercepting the light—none too abundant in any part of the church, though it is entirely destitute of stained glass at the present day.

The walls of the triforium and clerestory are perforated longitudinally to form a continuous passage on each side of the choir—interrupted, however, by the interposition of masonry at the junction of the lateral walls with the apse.

The passage along the clerestory is formed by a succession of "shouldered arches," as they are commonly called, though each merely consists of a flat lintel resting on corbels, which is not strictly an arch at all. As there are no signs of vaulting-shafts, it may be fairly assumed that the original roof was a wooden one, probably painted, like those still in existence at other Norman churches.

45 The present ceiling, about forty-seven feet above the level of the floor, is of panelled oak (uncoloured), and supersedes an unsatisfactory timber structure which had taken the place of the earlier Tudor work. It was divided into compartments by a tie-beam and king-post at intervals, supported on corbels representing the heads of cherubim—an innovation more modern, and even more out of character with the building, than the ceiling itself. The cross beams from the latter have been retained in the modern work.

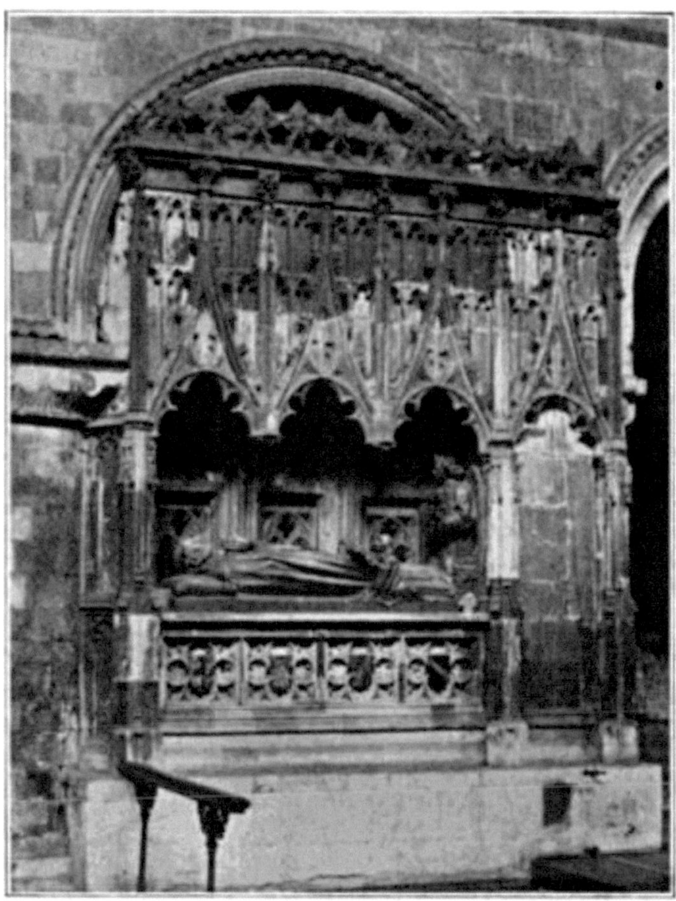

THE FOUNDER'S TOMB

46 **The Founder's Tomb** occupies a bay on the northern side of the sanctuary. Resting on a simple base of rectangular stones, it consists of an altar-tomb in the Perpendicular style, ornamented by four quatrefoil panels in front, each displaying a shield of arms, above which runs the inscription: *Hic jacet Raherus Primus Canonicus et Primus Prior hujus Ecclesiae.*

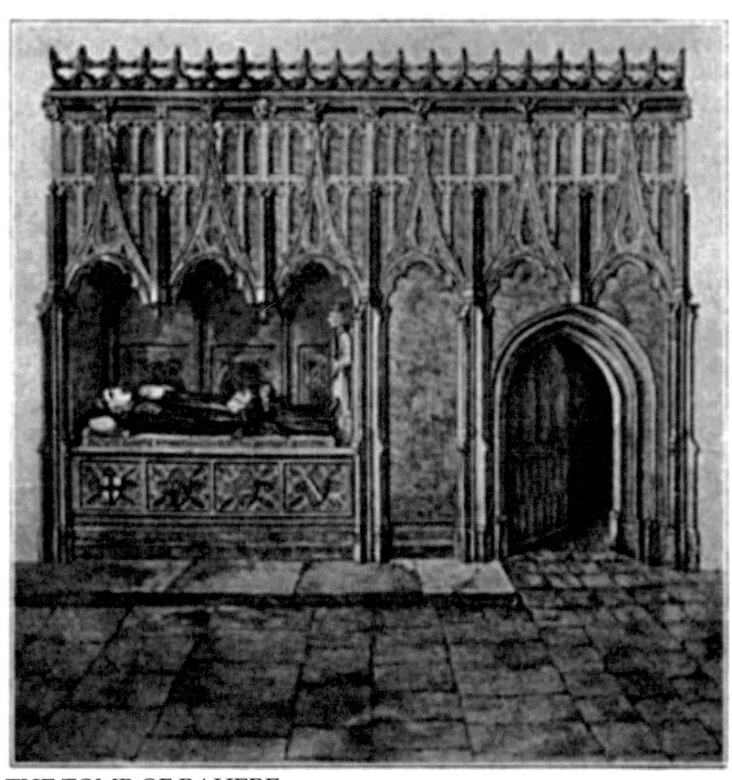

THE TOMB OF RAHERE
From an old engraving, showing the original extent of the arcaded work, and the doorway now removed

47 The painted effigy of Rahere lies upon its back, vested in the black Habit of the Augustinian Canons, the hands joined in prayer, and the tonsured head reposing upon a tasselled cushion. At the feet an angel, with flowing black hair, and crowned, is represented rising from clouds, holding towards the recumbent figure a shield, on which the Priory Arms are embossed and illuminated: *Gules*, two lions *passant guardant: or*, two ducal coronets in chief.

On each side of the effigy a kneeling monk of the same Order is reading from a book, opened at Isaiah, li, 3, as may be inferred from the words distinguishable on the page nearest the spectator, the text obviously having been chosen with reference to the ground on which the Priory stands: "Consolabitur ergo Dominus Sion, et consolabitur omnes ruinas ejus: et ponat desertum ejus quasi delicias, et solitudinem ejus quasi hortum Domini."

The group is enclosed in a canopied frame of tabernacle work in three divisions, elaborately carved, with a vaulted ceiling; and each of the panels in the back wall is perforated with a small decorated window, unglazed, probably inserted not only for ornament but for the benefit of pilgrims on the ambulatory side of the shrine. The design is continued in a fourth panel towards the east, with a blank wall behind it, and another separating it from the actual tomb. Originally there were two other panels beyond this, similarly arcaded, and carried over the face of the adjacent Norman arch, which had a doorway beneath it leading into the ambulatory (*see* illustration, p. 46). The canopy and panelling were added to the tomb in the fifteenth century. It was repaired in the reign of Henry VIII, and the painting has been more than once renewed, apparently with some rearrangement of the arms in front, as they do not appear in the present order in old engravings. Taking them from left to right they are now those of the City of London, the Priory, England and France, and Sir Stephen Slaney, Lord Mayor of London in 1595.

The sanctuary is paved with coloured tesserae and marbles, in a series of five steps, the uppermost of which forms the predella, or footpace, to the altar. The latter is of oak, and was presented by Miss Overbury, sister-in-law to the Rev. W. Panckridge, Rector of the Parish from 1884 to 1887.

The somewhat classical design of the pavement is uniform throughout, but the higher and lower portions are distinguished by separate inscriptions, one across the chord of the apse, the other along the step immediately within the railing. These inscriptions are respectively as follows:

To the Glory of God, and in memory of John Abbiss, 64 years Rector of this Church, this Apse was rebuilt by his nephew, Frederick P. Phillips, a.d. 1886. Let Thy priests be clothed with righteousness.

Where I am, there shall also my servant be.

48 In memory of the Rev. Canon F. Parr Phillips, Rector of Stoke d'Abernon, Surrey, and Patron of this Church. Died 17 March, 1903, aged 84.

Give unto the Lord the glory due unto His Name.
Bring an offering and come before Him.
Worship the Lord in the beauty of holiness. [4]

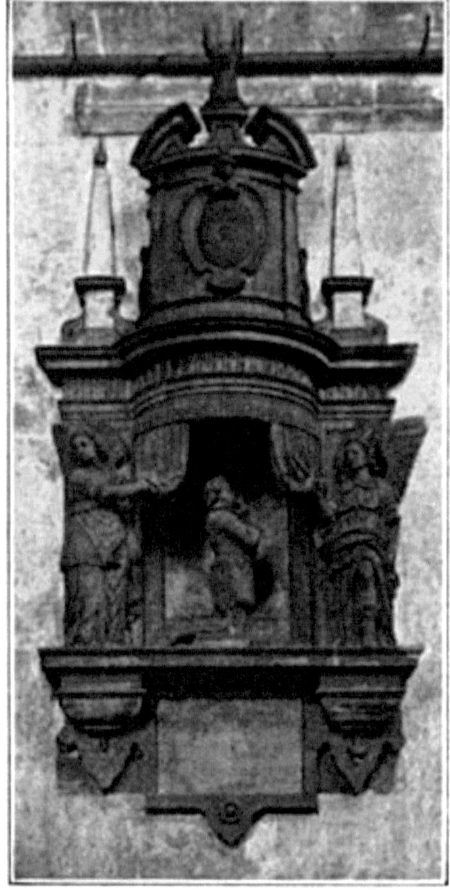

THE CHAMBERLAYNE MONUMENT

The Pulpit is built against a pier on the north side, midway between the ordinary seats and the choir-stalls. It is a low oblong structure, with a short flight of steps at each end, and is ornamented in the upper part with a series of panels, arcaded and perforated to resemble small windows.

49 The Hopton Wood stone, or marble, as it is sometimes called, has a delicate gray vein, which is brought out by polish on the cornice and balustrade, as a relief to the unpolished surface elsewhere displayed. There is no inscription; but visitors are usually told about Mrs. Charlotte Hart, the apparently impecunious pew-opener at the church, who surprised her friends by dying worth close upon £3,000, and by leaving £600 to the restoration fund. A new pulpit happened to be wanted at the time, and the bequest was applied in its erection.

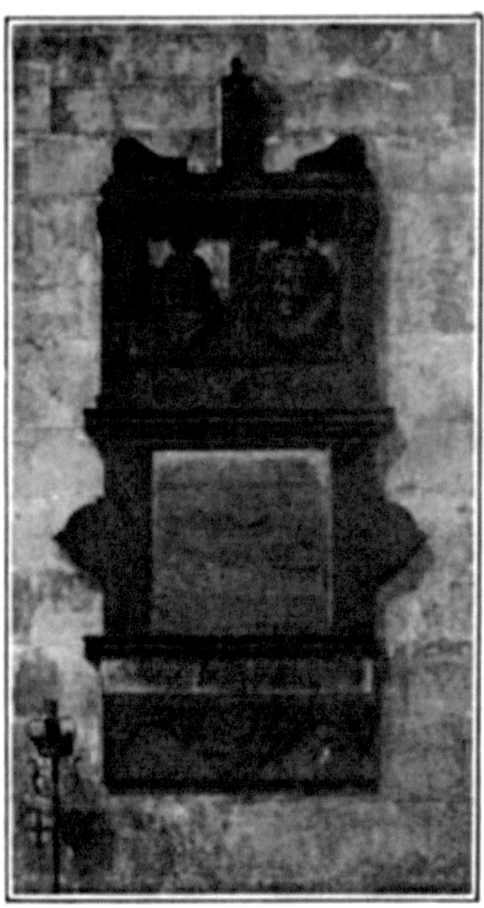

THE SMALPACE MONUMENT

50 On the wall above is the **Monument of Sir Robert Chamber-layne**, an elegant piece of Jacobean work, deserving a closer examination than can be bestowed upon it without mounting the pulpit, and even there the inscription is scarcely legible. The sculpture, which is extremely well executed, represents Sir Robert kneeling in prayer within a circular pavilion, the curtains of which are held up by an angel on either side. The figure wears a partial suit of plate armour over the costume of the period, and the (bearded) face is turned obliquely towards the east yet away from the spectator, in

the attitude of secret devotion. The tent is surmounted by a rich cornice, above which the monument terminates in an ornamental pediment displaying the crest of the deceased. The Latin inscription beneath relates his descent, through the holders of Sherburn Castle, Oxon, from the most ancient Tankerville family of Normandy; and adds that he was knighted by James I, and died between Tripoli and Cyprus, on a journey to the Holy Sepulchre, at the age of thirty-five, in the year 1615. The monument was erected by an unknown friend (*amico amicus*), who concludes with the pious ejaculation *Coelo tegitur qui non habet urnam*—Heaven covers him who has no sepulchre!

On the south wall, facing this monument, there is another of some interest and artistic merit. It is to the memory of **Percival Smalpace** and Agnes his wife, whose boldly sculptured heads are projecting from separate panels above the tablet containing the inscription. This is chiefly in Latin, and informs us that the deaths occurred respectively on 2nd February, 1568, and 3rd September, 1588, in the reign of Queen Elizabeth, and that Michael and Thomas erected the memorial jointly to the best of parents.

The moral of the English lines

Behold yourselves by us;
    Such once were we as you:
And you in time shall be
    Even dust as we are now.

is enforced by a drawing, in outline, representing the nude figures of the departed lying side by side upon a couch in the sleep of death—no doubt intended as a *memento mori* of a less repulsive kind than the usual desiccated corpse. The monument has been invested with a coating of black, which at once conceals the whole of the marble (said to be brown), and shows up the inscription and the figures, both clearly incised and gilded.

51 **The Ambulatory**, which encompasses the choir, and is open to it on the inner side throughout its course, is an interesting part of the original fabric, and displays to full advantage the characteristic features of early Norman work—here made more conspicuous by the low pitch of the roof, which gives the columns and arches an

appearance of even greater solidity than really belongs to them. The semicircular arches which support the roof spring from the capitals of the main arcade, and are merely wide bands of stone, without moulding or adornment of any kind. The intermediate spaces are equally plain, each compartment simply taking the quadripartite form (without vaulting-ribs) to accommodate it to the arcading on which it rests. The ceiling has been repaired with stone, and overlaid with plaster in the panels, but the design has been left undisturbed, as a specimen of early vaulting, rare enough to be worth preserving. 52 [5]

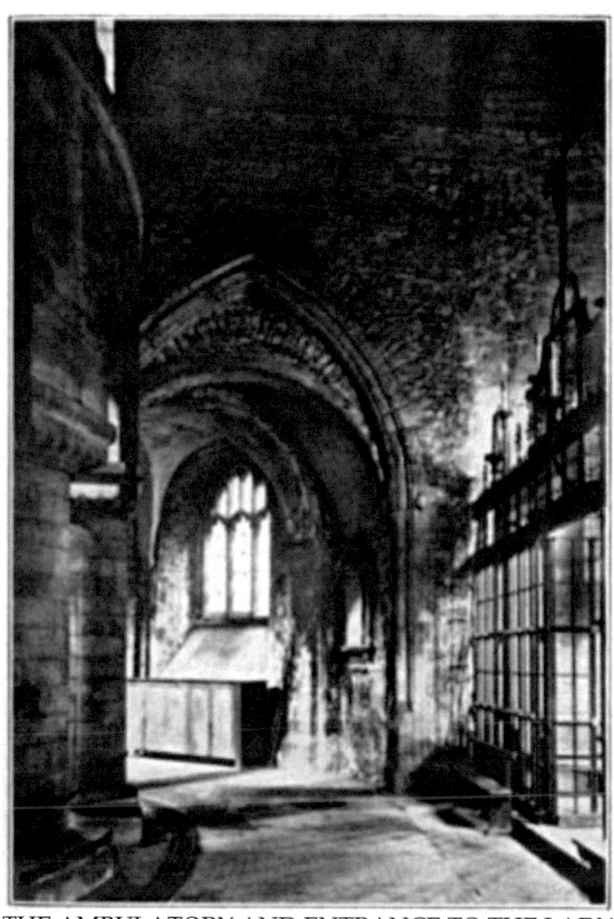

THE AMBULATORY AND ENTRANCE TO THE LADY CHAPEL

Perpendicular work occurs here and there throughout the ambulatory, conspicuously in the three recesses in the exterior wall on the north, each of which contains a three-light window in that style. The first and second of these recesses, or small chapels, are open to the ground level; but the third (nearest the east) has been walled up beneath the window sill. Beyond it is the door of the clergy vestry, which occupies the site of another chapel: and in the curve of the wall towards the Lady Chapel there is a tablet which usually attracts attention for the curious device upon it—three pillars

crowned by a garland of roses—and the poetical conceit of the epitaph, which explains the emblem, and otherwise speaks for itself:

Sacred

To the memory of that worthy and lerned

Francis Anthony, Doctor in Physick.

There needs no verse to beautify thy praise,

Or keepe in memory thy spotless name.

Religion, virtue, and thy skil did raise

A threefold pillar to thy lasting Fame;

Though poisenous envye ever sought to blame

Or hyde the fruits of thy intention,

Yet shall they all commend that high desygne

Of purest gold to make a medicine

That feel thy helpe by that thy rare invention.

He dyed the 26th of May 1623, of his age 74.

His loving sonne John Anthony, doctor in physick,

Left this remembrance of his sorrow. He dyed
y^e 28th April 1655, being aged 70 years, and was
buried nere this place, and left behind him 1 sone and
3 daughters. [6]

53

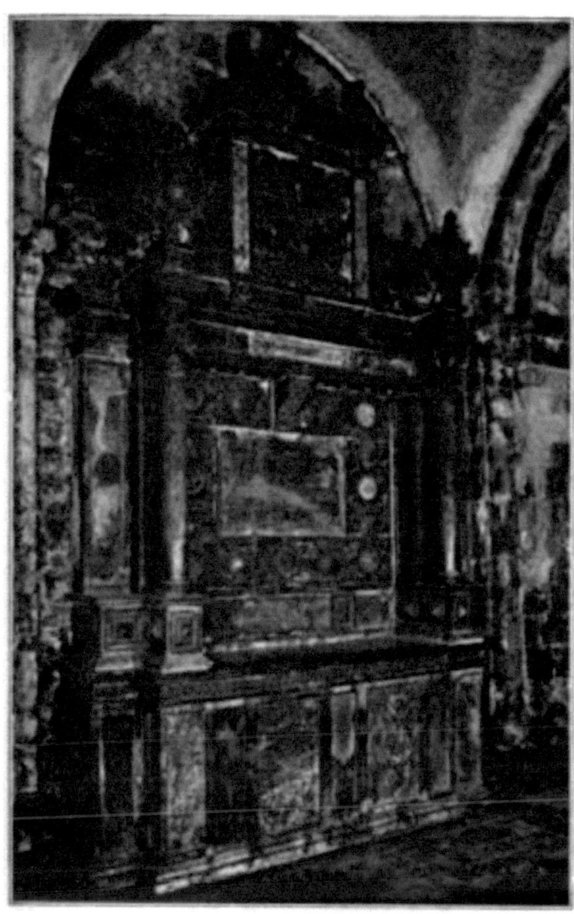

THE MILDMAY MONUMENT

54 Before leaving this northern side of the ambulatory it may be noticed that the pavement is made up of an intermixture of gravestones with encaustic tiles. The latter are not so old as they look, for they only date from 1863, when the floor was reduced to its original level, exactly twenty-seven inches below that which was removed, as shown by the marks on the wall backing Rahere's tomb, at the line where the pavement was taken away. The advantage as regards the proportions of the church is obvious enough; but a question has been opened as to whether the intermediate pavement was really so

modern as had been taken for granted. It is suggested to the contrary that it may have been first introduced during the Middle Ages, when the increasing veneration for the East required a greater elevation for that part of the church, to distinguish it from the less sacred nave, and give proper dignity to the High Altar and its surroundings. In some accounts it is positively stated that the floor was raised two feet six inches by Prior Bolton early in the sixteenth century.

55 Continuing our perambulation past the Lady Chapel and Prior Bolton's door (now leading into the choir vestry) at the eastern end of the south wall, we come to the magnificent **Tomb of Sir Walter Mildmay**. It formerly stood facing that of the Founder in the sanctuary, but was shifted to its present place in 1865, and renovated by Henry Bingham Mildmay in 1870, as stated in an inscription upon it, which, however, shows more signs of decay than any other part of the monument, and is scarcely legible. This very fine altar tomb is composed of various coloured marbles, panelled and gilded in a design combining the Elizabethan form with the classical ornament of the Renaissance, and is remarkable for the absence of figures usually conspicuous in monuments of the same age. This peculiarity is perhaps accounted for by the strong Puritan leanings of Sir Walter, who took no pains to conceal them in his lifetime. He founded Emmanuel College, Cambridge, in 1583, where his architectural work is pointed out, in illustration of his principles, as running counter to all the traditions of the Dominican Friars, whose buildings came into his hands after the Dissolution, and formed the nucleus of his foundation. Instead of saints and angels, or kneeling effigies, we have here eight shields of arms, showing the family alliances, arranged in panelling round the central inscription:

Hic jacent Gualterus Mildmay, miles, et
Maria uxor ejus. Ipse obiit ultimo die
Maii 1589. Ipsa 16 die Martii 1576.
Reliquierunt duos filios et tres filias.
Fundavit Collegium Emanuelis Cantabrigiae.
Moritur Cancellarius et Sub-Thesaurarius
Scaccarii et Regiae Majestati a Consiliis.

(= Here lie Walter Mildmay, Knight, and Mary his wife. He died the last day of May, 1589. She the 16th day of March, 1576. They left two sons and three daughters. He founded Emmanuel College, Cambridge. He died Chancellor and Sub-Treasurer of the Exchequer, and a Member of Her Majesty's Council.)

There is a commendable absence of eulogy in the epitaph, and, instead of any direct quotation from scripture, the motto, *Mors nobis lucrum* is given, as an adaptation of Phil. i, 21. The tomb is surmounted by three classical urns and the escutcheon of the deceased, with the legend, *Virtute non vi*. Sir Walter was one of the Royal Commissioners appointed in 1586 for the trial of Mary, Queen of Scots, at Fotheringhay Castle.

There are numerous other monuments in the church, and there were formerly many more than now remain, but those selected for description are the most important and the most interesting for their artistic merit.

The first rector of the parish, Sir John Deane, is commemorated in a modern brass (1893) let into the pavement of the ambulatory on the southern side of the chancel. It was inserted by the pupils of the Witton Grammar School, Northwich, founded by Sir John in the year 1557.

56 **The Lady Chapel** is a restoration of that built about the year 1410. At the Dissolution it passed into the hands of Sir Richard Rich, who converted it into a dwelling-house, and in more modern times it was occupied by a fringe manufacturer, as related in our historical sketch. The building was recovered by purchase in 1885, and the reconstruction begun, which was completed eleven years later. There are signs of an earlier chapel on the site, which was considerably altered, or entirely rebuilt, in the fourteenth century, as appeared from the architectural remains of that period discovered within the fifteenth-century fabric—itself in a frightful state of dilapidation—when the restoration was taken in hand.

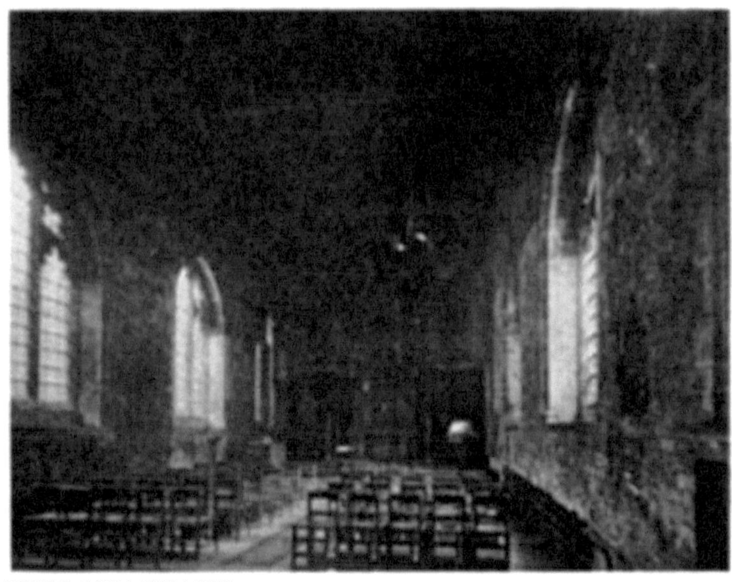

THE LADY CHAPEL

57 Though every care has been taken to preserve the old work, with a strict adherence to the general design, the greater part of the chapel is necessarily new. It is separated from the ambulatory by an elegant screen of ironwork, surmounted by a crucifix of white metal, which has been blackened into uniformity with the rest of the screen so that it can hardly be distinguished in the dim light. This characteristic of the church is preserved in the chapel by the omission of an east window. In place of it the wall-space above the altar is laid out in an arcading of five niches, with canopies and pedestals arranged in parallel lines, providing for a double row of statues, not yet inserted. The lower part of the wall is curtained, with a small canopy over the altar, containing an oil painting of the Virgin and Child as an appropriate form of reredos. There are three rather large windows on each side, of which those on the south are entirely new, but the sills and jambs on the north show a retention of fifteenth-century work. This appears again in the walls on either side of the sanctuary, each of which contains an arcaded recess of three divisions (the central glazed), those on the south forming the sedilia. The sanctuary is paved with Roman tesserae and coloured marbles,

in agreement with the pavement beneath the High Altar, but of a less elaborate pattern. [7]

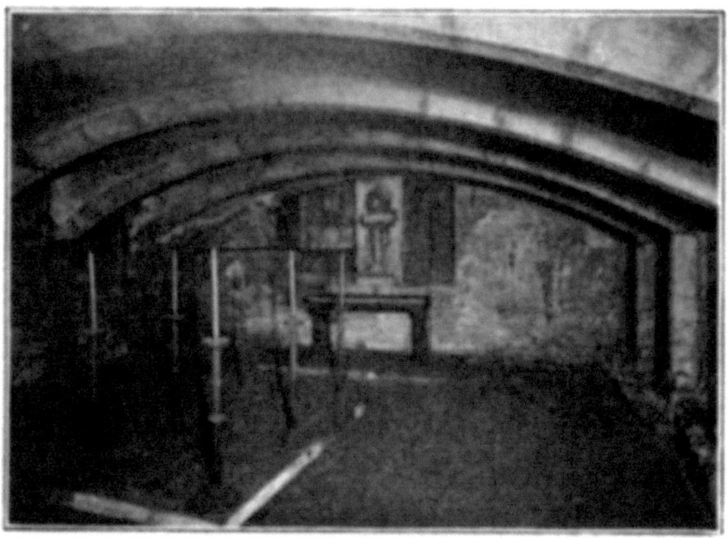

THE CRYPT

58 **The Crypt** beneath the Lady Chapel has no internal connection with it, but is entered by an outside door in the south wall. Like the rest of the Priory buildings it has gone through many vicissitudes. Obviously built at the same time as the chapel, it is supposed to have been used originally as a receptacle for the bones exhumed from time to time in the neighbouring canons' cemetery. Passing into secular hands at the Dissolution, it was partly filled up with earth, and then used as a coal and wine cellar to the dwelling-house above, and eventually formed part of the manufactory before mentioned, the marks of which have been left here and there upon the walls. The little building is now equipped as a mortuary chapel, with an altar against the east wall, and an oblong space marked off on the floor before it, with the usual lateral candlesticks, for the reception of a corpse. As a general rule, however, the funeral services are held in the choir, where there are greater facilities. Though extremely simple, the architectural features are very interesting, the old work having been retained in the walls, piers, and windows, the vaulting alone being new. This merely consists of depressed arches,

carried across from the north to the south wall, the intermediate spaces being overlaid with plaster.

At the eastern end, above the altar, one of the window recesses has the socket of an old iron hinge within it, and otherwise shows signs of having been formerly occupied by a door, which may possibly have been the original entrance. It is supposed that all the windows were left unglazed for the sake of ventilation, but plain glass is now inserted. The recesses are very deeply splayed in the thickness of the walls, and it will be noticed that the exterior openings are above the level of the roof, so as to admit the daylight obliquely, an ingenious contrivance to intensify the solemnities within, where an artificial light is almost a necessity. The plain bands of stone which constitute the vaulting are supported by shallow piers, or pilasters, built against the lateral walls, and all alike in their general structure and moulded bases; but there is a curious difference between those on the north and south, which has given rise to some antiquarian speculation. In one case (the north) the pilasters are carried down to the floor: in the other they rest upon a stone plinth or skirting a few inches above it.

59 **The Cloister**, as next in importance to the church itself, and so characteristic of a monastic foundation as to give a name to the whole, was in all probability begun by Rahere, or at least some time in the twelfth century. This may be inferred from the Norman work found and preserved at the restoration—at present confined to three bays of the eastern side, at right angles to the south wall of the church. The cloister was originally continued parallel with this wall to the extremity of the nave, whence it extended in the usual quadrangular form, each side consisting of eight bays, enclosing the area known as the cloister-garth. That there was a reconstruction under Prior John Watford, early in the fifteenth century, is clear from the evidence already given, which is confirmed by the architectural remains within the restored fragment—all that was in existence, as a ruin, when the renovation was attempted.

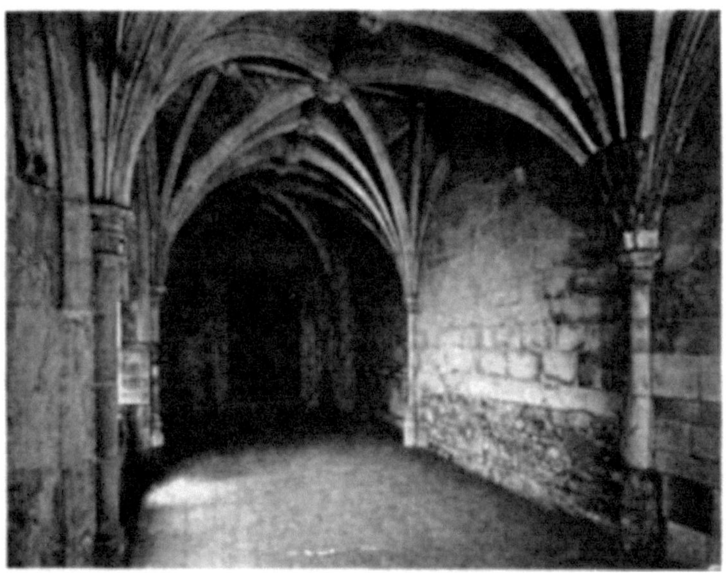

THE REMAINING BAYS OF THE CLOISTER

60 The entrance is through a round-headed doorway in the south aisle—an interesting piece of Norman work—but the doors are probably those inserted during the fifteenth century reconstruction. It seems that they were taken out when the nave was destroyed, and fitted to the main entrance in the wall then built at the west end. Subsequently stored within the church among the lumber which might possibly come in useful, they were found exactly to fit the opening into the cloister, where they were re-hung in what seems to be their proper place. The first bay on the right, which formerly opened into the northern side of the quadrangle, is now occupied by a blank wall, with some fifteenth century work on each side, and the Tudor door-jambs within it, supposed to have been inserted by the Dominican Friars in their restoration of the following century. The second and third bays contain windows, with very fine modern tracery in the headings, and some old Perpendicular work retained at the sides. The wall on the left (eastern) side shows a similar intermixture of styles in its three unlighted bays. The elaborately vaulted roof is for the most part new, but a few of the old bosses, and some portions of the original vaulting-shafts recovered

during the excavations, have been incorporated into it, without renovation of their surfaces, so that the ancient and modern can be easily distinguished. The new bosses are sculptured with shields bearing respectively the royal arms, the arms of the Diocese, the Priory, the late Rector (Sir Borradaile Savory), and the City of London. The Priory arms form the central point in the vaulting, surrounded by smaller bosses containing the emblems of the four Evangelists.

On a table at the end of the cloister there is a small collection of stones and encaustic tiles from the old building, and some more precious relics in a case. These include a few broken pieces of stained glass, the metal seal struck by Father Perrin for the Dominicans, a book of "Spiritual Exercises" by the same Prior, and a charred fragment of Rahere's coffin and sandal, which had been surreptitiously taken from his tomb.

Before leaving the church, the visitor is recommended to look through the scrap-book of old engravings in charge of the verger, showing the buildings in various phases of their history since the Dissolution. These interesting pictures were presented anonymously, but a note on the fly-leaf by Dr. Norman Moore, dated 23rd May, 1885, informs us that the donor was William Morrant Baker, F.R.C.S., Surgeon to St. Bartholomew's Hospital, Lecturer on Physiology, and Warden of its College. There is a tablet to his memory in the Church of St. Bartholomew-the-Less.

61 A special permit is required for an inspection of the church registers. They date from 1616, and show an average death-rate of ten in each month till the year 1665, when the Plague of London brought up the entries to about eighteen on each day.

62 The interior of the church presents an interesting perspective from almost any point. A good general view may be obtained from the north-east or south-west corner, and another from the organ-gallery, which is recommended as commanding features not well seen from below in the scanty light.

FOOTNOTES

[1] This altar is an interesting piece of (Jacobean?) woodwork which has recently been uncovered. The low recess in which it

stands seems better suited for a tomb, or recumbent effigy, while the more lofty recess against the eastern wall, originally supposed to have been open to the Walden Chantry, would hold the altar admirably, and give it the proper orientation.

[2] There are two large canvases of his on the staircase of the Hospital representing "The Pool of Bethesda" and "The Good Samaritan," besides four smaller paintings, one of which gives "Rahere's Dream," and another "The Building of the Priory."

[3] The manor of Canonbury, formerly included in the Priory estates, is said to have been presented to the community by Sir Ralph de Berners in the reign of Edward III. The Prior and canons built themselves a mansion there as a country residence, and there is no doubt that the place takes its name from their connection with it. According to Stow (*Ed. Strype*, vol. 1), the manor-house was rebuilt by Prior Bolton, whose rebus on the walls of the tower seemed to prove that it was either his work, or erected shortly after his time to his memory. The house is a plain brick structure with gable ends, and the tower (of the same material) covers a rather large square. The spacious rooms within it have some literary interest, as at one time occupied by Ephraim Chambers, the encyclopaedist (1680-1750), and by the more famous Oliver Goldsmith. The whole building, renovated within and without, is now held by a social club. For many years a fable was believed that a subterranean passage connected it with the Smithfield Priory.

[4] The new bronze railing to the sanctuary forms part of the memorial to the late Rector, the Rev. Sir Borradaile Savory, Bart. It is in the Renaissance style, and the words from the *Gloria in Excelsis* ("We praise Thee," etc.), in each of its four divisions, were selected by his successor, the present Rector, as suitable to the place, and expressing the governing principle of Sir Borradaile's life, as well as that of Rahere the Founder.

[5] The substructure in the chamber of the Pix, at Westminster, will be remembered among the surviving examples of this early kind of vaulting in England.

[6] Francis Anthony (1550-1623) lived in Bartholomew Close. He had obtained the M.A. degree at Cambridge, but none in medicine, and having practised for six months in London without a licence, he

was summoned before the President and Censors of the College of Physicians to give an account of himself. Failing to satisfy his examiners, he was interdicted from practice, but ignored the prohibition, and suffered more than one imprisonment in consequence. The medicine "of purest gold" was a panacea, known as *Aurum potabile*, which was supposed to be made from the precious metal, and certainly put a great deal of it into the inventor's pocket, as a fashionable remedy for all kinds of diseases.

(See article in the "Dictionary of National Biography" for a sketch of his life.)

[7] A tablet, in the Renaissance style, has recently been affixed to the north wall in memory of Sir Borradaile Savory, Bart., the late Rector. It was unveiled and formally dedicated by the Bishop of Stepney, on Sunday, 10th May, 1908.

63

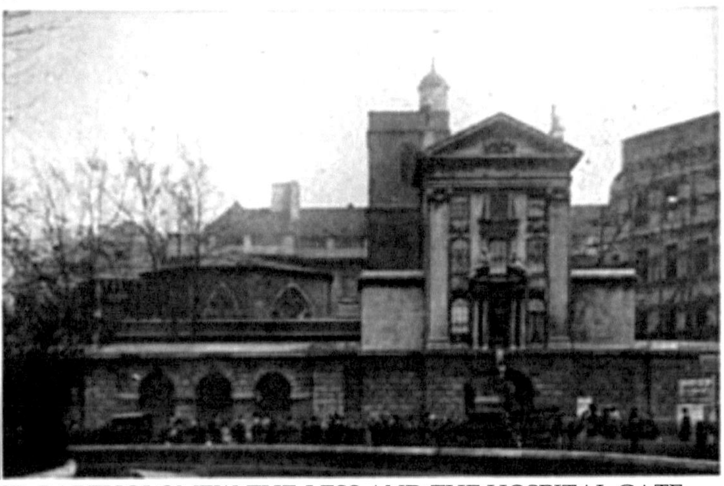

ST. BARTHOLOMEW-THE-LESS AND THE HOSPITAL GATE
Table of
Contents
64

CHAPTER IV

ST. BARTHOLOMEW-THE-LESS AND THE HOSPITAL

Visitors to Rome will remember the Isola Tiberina, which lies in a curve of the river between the city and Trastevere, and is reached from the respective sides by the Ponte Quattro Capi and the Ponte San Bartolomeo. It was to the hospital on this island that Rahere was sent for medical treatment in his illness; and it is possible that the disposing cause of his vision, with its practical outcome, may be found in the circumstances of the place. The island had been dedicated to Aesculapius on the strength of an ancient Roman legend; and about the year 1000 the Emperor Otho III, erected a Christian church there—probably on the site of a temple to the god—which was named after St. Bartholomew, on the supposition that it contained the saint's relics. [1] Below the church there are the remains of the old travertine ramparts which gave the island the appearance of a ship on which the edifice was resting—a fanciful picture of the "Navis Ecclesiae" as reproduced in the twelfth century Priory seal. (*Vide* Fig. C, page 73) The combination of a hospital with a church, suggested by the island and the vision, was realized in Rahere's double foundation on his return to England. Until the time of the Dissolution the corporate body of the hospital, and the staff for attendance upon the patients, were identical, and consisted of a master, eight brethren, and four sisters, all living in obedience to the Augustinian rule. Unfortunately no record is preserved of the grant of the site, or of the deed of endowment; but a Charter granted by Henry I in 1133 is extant, conferring certain privileges on the church, prior, canons, and poor of the hospital. (*Vide ante* chap. i.) The annexation of the hospital to the priory was subsequently confirmed by a Charter of King John in the fifth year of his reign, which remained in force without material change till the separation effected under Henry VIII. The connection involved the presentation of each newly elected Master to the Prior of St. Bartholomew's, or, if he refused institution, to the Bishop of London; the assent of the prior and canons being, however, required before any one could become a member of the Hospital Society. The Act of 1539 superseded all previous legislation affecting the monastic foundations; the Priory and Hospital were separated; and the revenues of both transferred to the royal exchequer. But on the petition of Sir Richard Gresham, Lord Mayor of London, and father of Sir Thomas Gresham, the Hospital was refounded by royal charter—27th December, 1546, 38 Henry VIII—which restored the greater part of its former revenues, in consideration of

the miserable estate of the poore, aged, sick, low, and impotent people, as well men as women, lying and going about begging in the common streets of the said City of London and the suburbs of the same, to the great paine and sorrowe of the same poore, aged, sick, and impotent people, and to the great infection, hurt, and annoyance of His Grace's loving subjects, which of necessity must daily goe and pass by the same poore, sick, low, and impotent people, being infected with divers great and horrible sicknesses and diseases.

65

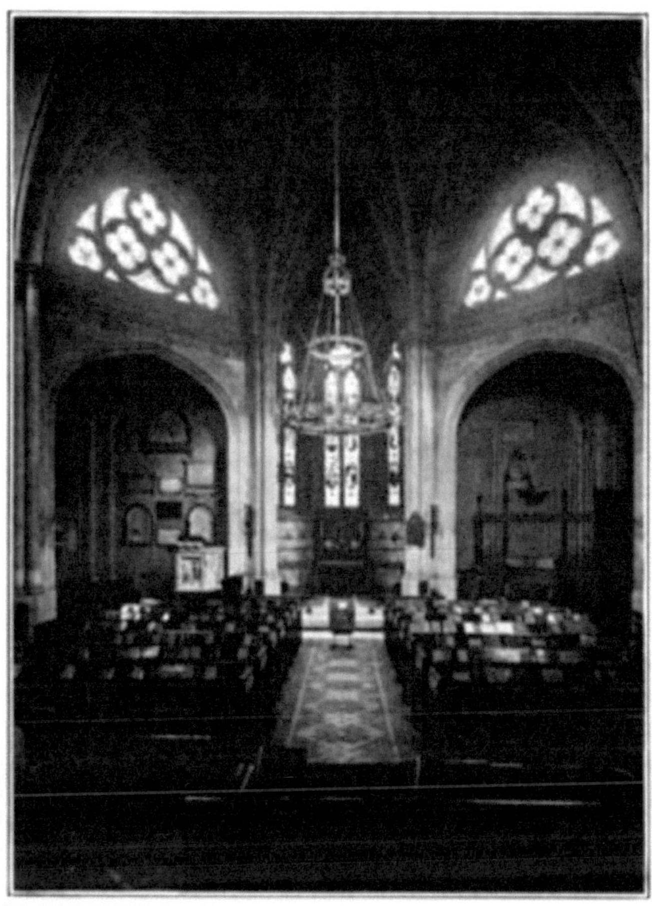

ST. BARTHOLOMEW-THE-LESS

The Indenture goes on to convey to the mayor, commonalty, and citizens of London the buildings formerly belonging to the Grey Friars as well as

the late Hospital of St. Bartholomew, in West Smithfield, otherwise called the Hospital of Little St. Bartholomew, and the Church of the same, and all the manors, parsonages, messuages, lands, tithes, advowsons, and hereditaments, late part of the possession of the said Hospital

66 with certain specified exceptions which the charity had to lose, and no longer form part of its history. The immediate result was that the Church of the Grey Friars became the parish church of Christ Church, Newgate, and the chapel pertaining to the hospital (the survivor of four, three of which were alienated) the parish church of Little St. Bartholomew, now more familiarly known as St. Bartholomew-the-Less. Two priests were then attached to it, one called the vicar, who was granted a mansion and a stipend of *£13 6s. 8d.* per annum; the other, the hospitaller or visitor, whose stipend was fixed at *£10.* The accommodation of the hospital at that time was for one hundred poor men and women, lodging within it, under the superintendence of a single matron, with twelve women assistants. It is interesting to compare these figures with those of the present day, when the hospital contains as many as six hundred and seventy beds, with three hundred and fifty nurses on the staff, and every year relieves over one hundred and fifty thousand poor sick people, besides maintaining a convalescent home, with seventy beds, at Kettlewell, Swanley, Kent. [2]

67 The hospital chapel, converted into a parish church after the Dissolution, had fallen into a very dilapidated state towards the end of the eighteenth century. In the year 1789 the restoration of the building was committed to Mr. George Dance, then architect and surveyor to the hospital. He made a considerable alteration in the interior by ruthlessly destroying the old work, for which he substituted an octagonal structure, within the rectangular plan, allowing the external walls to remain in their original form, with the square tower which still stands at the western end — the whole enveloped in a coating of cement. The internal erection was entirely in wood, ingeniously carved and coloured to resemble stone; but the false economy of it was soon manifested in dry-rot, which spread to such an alarming extent that a reconstruction became necessary. The rebuilding was taken in hand in 1823 by Mr. Thomas Hardwick, who had a much better knowledge of pointed architecture than his predecessor. He removed the whole of the timber, substituting stone and iron for it, and while adhering to Mr. Dance's general design, improved upon it by introducing fresh details of his own, more in harmony with the fabric in which it was enclosed. The church has since been restored, but the incongruity is still obvious

enough, especially from the outside, where the octagon projects above the ancient walls, and the small pentagonal chancel beyond them at the eastern end.

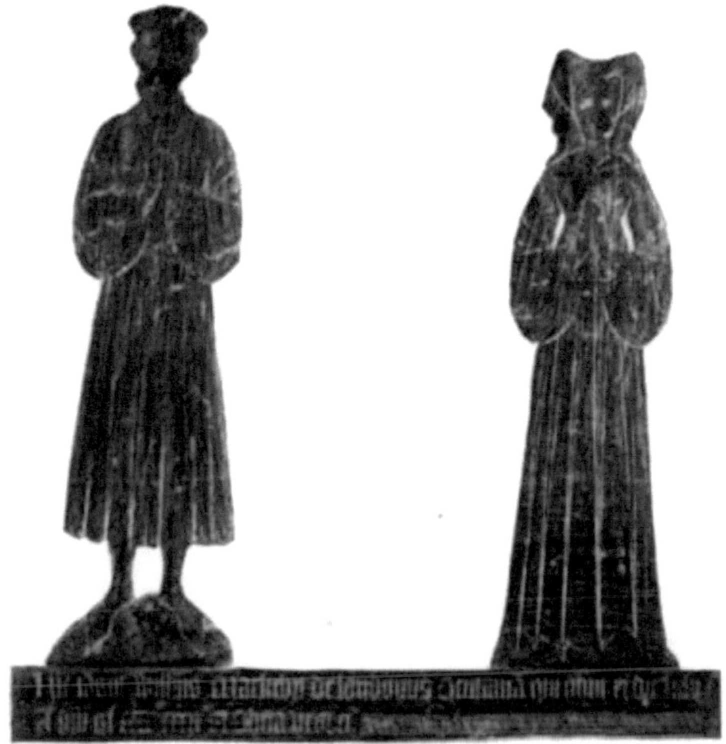

BRASS OF WILLIAM AND ALICE MARKEBY

68 The entrance is by a low Tudor doorway in the tower, which still bears traces of the original work. On the pavement of the vestibule there is an interesting brass, with the figures of William Markeby and his wife, and an inscription which now reads: "Hic jacent Will'mo Markeby de Londiniis gentlemo' qui obiit XI die Julii A. D'ni MCCCCXXXIX et Alicia uxor ei," the concluding words "quorum animabus propitietur Deus. Amen" having been erased. [3] There are two other ancient memorials in this part of the church which call for special notice, viz.: on the north wall, within the present vestry, a niche contains the figure of an angel bearing a shield

of arms, beneath which another shield, surmounted by a crown, and upheld by two angels, displays the arms of Edward the Confessor impaled with those of England. And against the western wall there is a good example of a canopied altar-tomb, in the Tudor style, with a memorial tablet (1741) inserted in it, which is obviously much later than the tomb itself. This is said to have originally stood at the eastern end of the south wall, where it was discovered during the eighteenth century reconstruction, and then deprived of its ornamental projections, where the marks of the chisel are seen upon the surface.

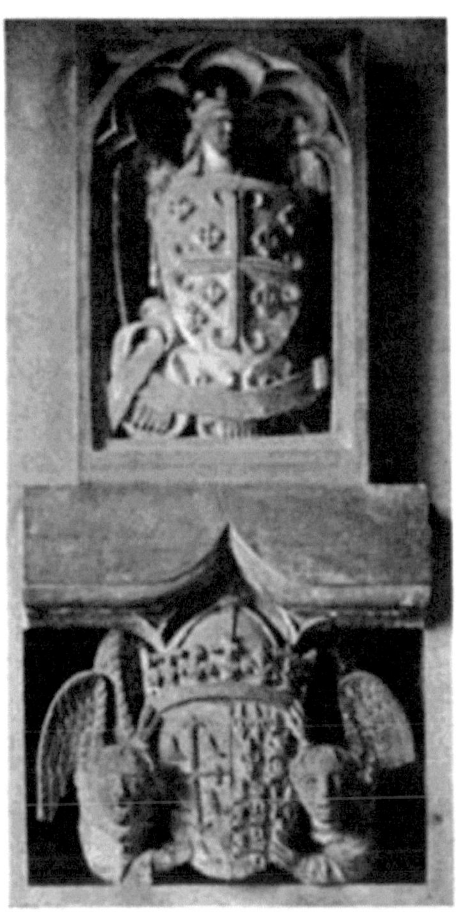

ANCIENT SCULPTURED TABLETS IN ST. BARTHOLOMEW-
THE-LESS WEST END OF NORTH WALL

69 At the eastern end of the north wall there is a tablet to the memory of the wife of Sir Thomas Bodley, whose name has been given to the famous library at Oxford. The curious old stone beneath it, which was discovered during the alterations, and then affixed to the wall, has the double interest of great antiquity and a puzzling inscription beginning, *"Ecce sub hoc tumulo Guliemus conditur."*

The exterior of the church, though spoilt by the composition laid over the walls, has still a certain interest as part of the original fabric, and still contains the arches of most of the old windows, viz., three on each side, one at the west end, another immediately over the doorway, and four in the uppermost storey of the tower. There were originally four windows on each side, but those in the easternmost bays have been removed, and the spaces filled up. Besides containing the memorials above mentioned, the vestibule has more architectural interest than any other part of the building in the surviving arches on the northern and eastern sides of the space beneath the tower. Here there is an aggregation of columns, with moulded bases and capitals, and banded in the centre, varied by the introduction of half-length shafts resting on sculptured corbels. The central area is nearly square, but has been formed into an octagon by an arcading, on a series of clustered columns, from each of which spring the moulded ribs of the ceiling. These ribs are of Bath stone, and after an elaborate intertwining, are brought together above in a central boss, from which hangs a large brass corona to light the church. The roof is of iron, the panels within the groining being overlaid with plaster. Above the main arcade there is a clerestory of dwarfed windows, filled with tinted glass in an ornamental framework, as are also the side windows, excepting those nearest the east. These display a selection of Scripture miracles. There are three painted windows over the altar, the central containing scenes from the life of Christ, those to the north and south representing the Old and New Testaments respectively. To the north of the recess forming the sanctuary there is an alabaster pulpit, [4] and on the south stands a small organ.

70 Services are held at eleven and five o'clock on Sundays, and the church is open every day for private devotion. It is provided with seats to accommodate about 200 people. The present vicar and hospitaller is the Rev. Herbert Skillicorn Close, M.A.

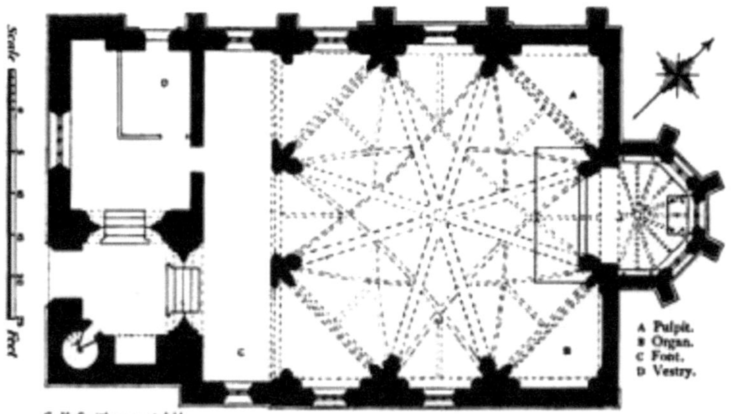

PLAN OF ST. BARTHOLOMEW-THE-LESS

Dimensions: length, including vestibule, 65 ft.; without vestibule, 50 ft.; width, 41 ft. 9 in.

(The measurements do not include the small chancel.)

FOOTNOTES

[1] St. Bartholomew was first interred at Albanopolis, in Greater Armenia, the scene of his passion, and his remains were afterwards translated successively to Daras, a city on the confines of Persia; to the island of Lipari; and to Beneventum. There is a tradition that his relics were eventually conveyed to Rome, but exactly where they were laid is uncertain.

[2] A full account of the hospital, brought down to 1837, is given in the Report of the Charity Commissioners on "Charities in England," issued in that year (*vide* No. 32, part vi), and since reprinted by Messrs. Wyman and Sons. Dr. Norman Moore is now engaged in writing a new history to the present time. The name of the first patient is recorded in the "Liber Fundationis" as "Adwyne of Dunwych."

[3] At the time of Stow's survey the church contained many brasses and monuments which have disappeared; but a tolerably complete account of them may be obtained by adding the descriptions supplied by Weever ("Funeral Monuments") and Gough ("Sepulchral Monuments," vol. ii) to those given by the old chronicler.

[4] There was formerly a chapel in the north-east corner.

APPENDIX I

THE PRIORY SEALS

Fig. A. Twelfth century. Sulphur cast from fine impression, the edge chipped. About 3-1/8 × 2 in. when perfect.

Pointed oval: St. Bartholomew standing, with nimbus, lifting up the right hand in benediction, in the left hand a long cross.

... HOSPITALIS SANCTI ... HOLOME ...

(3487. lxviii. 45.)

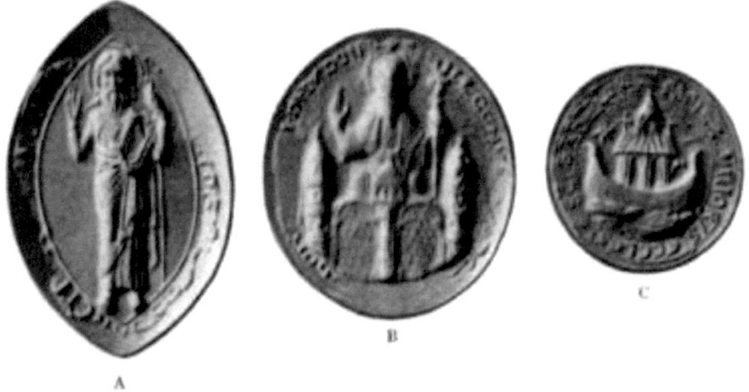

Fig. B. Twelfth century. Sulphur cast from imperfect impression. About 2½ × 2¼ in. when perfect.

Oval: St. Bartholomew, with nimbus, lifting up the right hand in benediction, in the left hand a long cross. The saint is half length on the section of a church, with round-headed arches, and two circular side-towers.

✠SIGILL' CONVENTUS ECC ... HOLO ... I. DE. LVDON.

(3488. lxviii. 22.)

74 Fig. C. A Counterseal. Twelfth century. Sulphur cast, 1¾ in. A church, with central tower, a cross at each gable end, and two tall round-headed arches in the wall, standing on a ship of antique shape, with curved prow and stern, each terminating in a bird's head, on the sea. In a field over the tower, the inscription: NAVIS ECCL'IE. On the left a wavy estoile of six points, on the right a crescent.

SIG-
ILL':PRIORIS:ECCLESIE:SCI:BARTOLOMEI.

(3489. lxviii. 23.)

Fig. D. Later Seal. Thirteenth and fourteenth centuries. Sulphur cast from imperfect impression. About 3 × 1 7 /8 in.

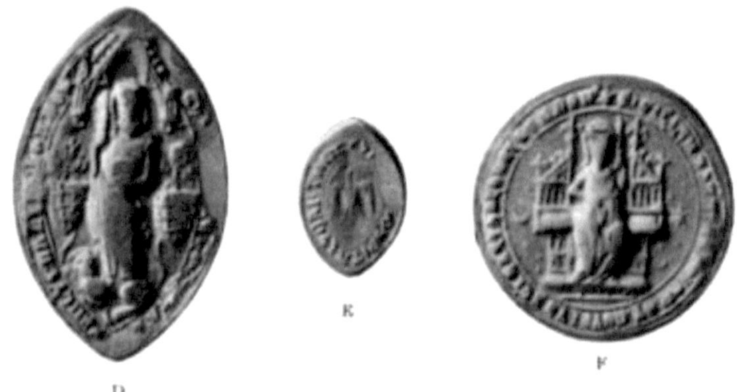

Pointed oval: St. Bartholomew standing on a lion *couchant guardant*, in the right hand a knife, his emblem, in the left hand a book. Overhead, a trefoil canopy pinacled and crocketed. On each side in the field a tree on which is slung by the strap a shield of arms: England.

S'C ... E. HOSPITAL ... SANCTI:BARTH'I.
LONDON'.

(3490. lxviii. 46.)

Fig. E. A Counterseal. Thirteenth century. Sulphur cast from chipped impression. 1¼ × 7/8 in.

Pointed oval: the impression of an antique oval intaglio gem. An eagle displayed.

✠SI ... HOSPITAL'. S. BARTHOL'.

(3491. lxviii. 47.)

75

Fig. F. Common Seal of the Prior and Convent. A.D. 1533. Bronze-green: fine, showing marks of the pins or studs employed to keep the two sides of the matrix in proper position, 2-1/8 in.

Obverse. St. Bartholomew, seated on a carved throne (somewhat resembling the throne on the *obv.* of the great seal of Edward I), in the right hand a book, in the left hand a knife. In the field, on the left a crescent, on the right an estoile, each between two groups of three small spots (the whole representing the heavens). Thirteenth century style of work.

✿SIGILLVM : COMMVNE : PRIOR' : ET : COVETV[S : SCI : BA]RTHOLOMEI : LONDON'.

(3492 and *Harl. Ch.* 83 A. 43.)

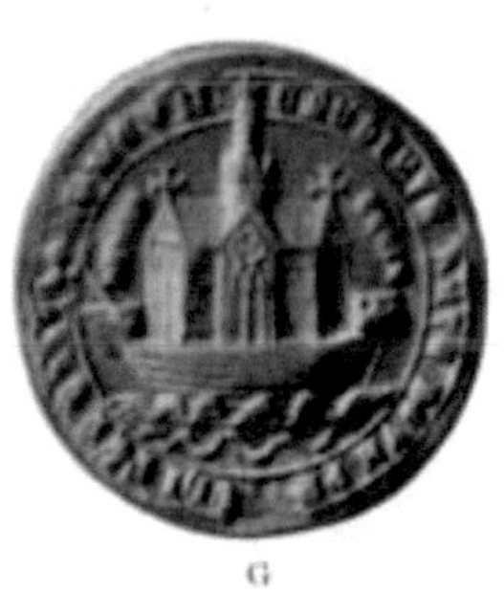
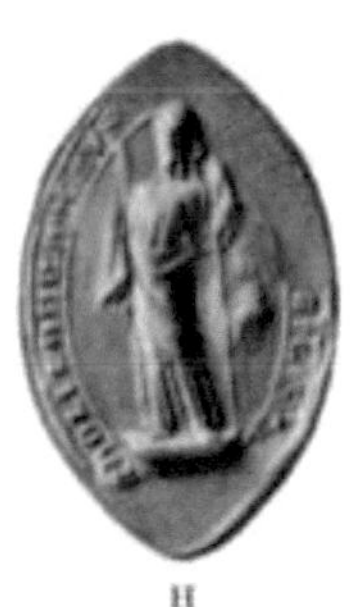
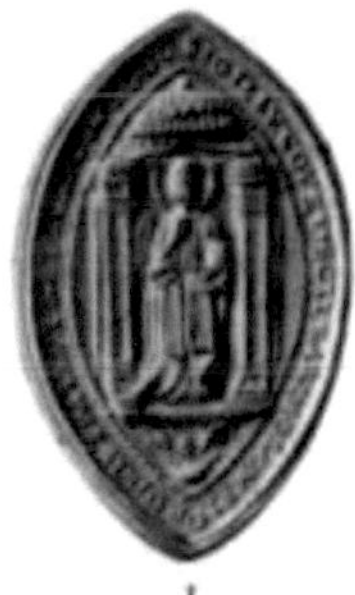

G H I

Fig. G. Reverse of the same seal. A church, with central spire, a cross at each gable end, masoned walls imitating ashlar-work, and traceried windows, standing on a ship with a castle at each end, that on the left pointed, that on the right square, on the sea.

In the field at the sides, the inscription:

NAVIS ECCL'E. CREDIMVS : ANTE : DEVM :
PROVEHI : PER : BARTHOLOMEVM.

Beaded borders. ("Vetusta Monumenta," vol. ii, pl. xxxvi.)

76 *Fig. H. Seal ad Causas.* Fourteenth century. Sulphur cast from imperfect impression. 2-3/8 × 1½ in.

Pointed oval: St. Bartholomew standing on a corbel, in the right hand a knife, in the left hand a long cross.

... ET CONV ... THOL'I LOND' AD CAVS ...

(3495. lxviii. 26.)

Fig. I. Seal of the New Foundation for Preaching Friars, by Queen Mary. A.D. 1556-1558. 2½ x 1-5/8 in.

Pointed oval: St. Bartholomew, standing, with nimbus, in the right hand a knife, in the left hand a book, under a dome-shaped baldachin or canopy in the style of the Renaissance, supported on two pilasters. In the exergue a floral ornament.

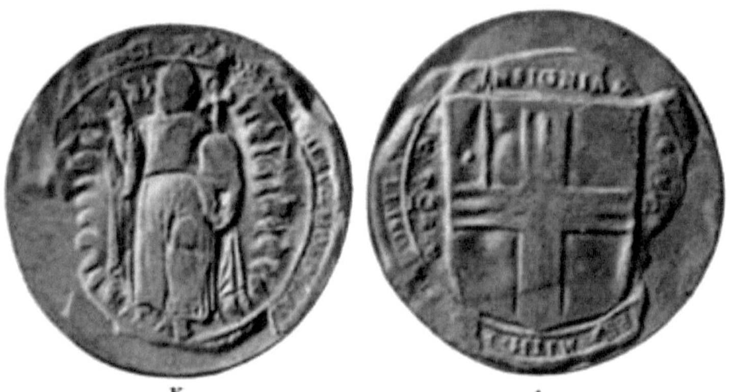

SIGILLV. COVET' SCTI : BARTHOLOMEI :
ORDINIS

FRATRV PREDICATORV : LODO.

Inner border beaded.

(From an impression taken direct from the matrix in the Church. There is an example on red sealing-wax in the British Museum. — 3496. XXV. 88; see also "Archaeologia," vol. XV, p. 400.)

Later Seal of the Hospital.

A.D. 1695. Red, covered with paper before impression. 3 in.

(3498, and Add. Ch. 1685.)

77 *Fig. K. Obverse.* St. Bartholomew, full-length, surrounded with radiance, lifting up the right hand in benediction, in the left hand a long cross.

✠COMM ... SIGILLV HOSPITAL' APOSTOLI.

Fig. L. Reverse. A shield of arms: City of London.

In the field, the inscriptions: 1[66]1 (?). INSIGNIA LONDO.

Background diapered with wavy branches of foliage.

... EST SMITHFIELD ⚜ET ⚜HOSPITALI ...

With the exception of the Marian seal (Fig. *I*), the illustrations come from the impressions in the British Museum, whose catalogue numbers are given in every case for convenient reference.

Table of
Contents

APPENDIX II

THE AUGUSTINIAN PRIORS

Rahere	1123-1144
Thomas	1144-1174
Roger	about 1174
Richard	1202-1206
G. of Osney	1213
John	1226-1232
Gerard	1232-1241
Peter le Duc	1242-1255
Robert	1255-1261
Gilbert de Weledon	1261-1263
John Bacun	1265
Henry	
Hugh	1273-1295
John de Kensington	1295-1316
John de Pekenden	1316-1350
Edmund de Broughyng	1350-1355
John de Carleton	1355-1361
Thomas de Watford	1361-1382
William Gedeney	1382-1391
John Eyton, D.D., *alias* Repyngdon	1391-1404
John Watford	1404-1414
William Coventre	1414-1436
Reginald Colier	1436-1471
Richard Pulter	1471-1480
Robert Tollerton	1480-1484

William Guy   1484-1505

William Bolton   1505-1532

Robert Fuller, Abbot of Waltham   1532-1539

Priory suppressed, 31 Henry VIII   25th October, 1539

Priory revived, 2 and 3 Philip and Mary   Easter, 1556

Dominican Prior

William Perrin, D.D.   1556-1558

Priory suppressed, I Elizabeth   13th July, 1559

Rectors

John Deane   { Parish Priest   1539-1544
                      Rector   1544-1563

Ralph Watson   1565-1569

Robert Binks   1570-1579

James Stancliffe, M.A.   1581

John Pratt   1582-1587

David Dee, M.A.   1587-1605

Thomas Westfield, D.D., Bishop of Bristol   1605-1644

John Garrett, M.A.   1644-1655

Randolph Harrison, D.D.   1655-1663

Anthony Burgess, M.A.   1663-1709

John Poultney, M.A.   1709-1719

Thomas Spateman, M.A.   1719-1738

Richard Thomas Bateman   1738-1761

John Moore, M.A.   1761-1768

Owen Perrott Edwardes, M.A.   1768-1814

John Richard Roberts, B.D.   1814-1819

John Abbiss, M.A.   1819-1883

William Panckridge, M.A.   1884-1887

Sir Borradaile Savory, Bart., M.A.   1887-1906

William Fitzgerald Gambier Sandwith, M.A.   1907

Patron of the Living

Capt. F. A. Phillips.

APPENDIX III

INVENTORY OF VESTMENTS, ETC.,
AT THE CHURCH OF ST. BARTHOLOMEW-THE-GREAT,
TAKEN IN THE YEAR 1574

"Certayne things appertaining to the Churche as followethe: —

- Imprimis a comunion cloth of redd silke and goulde.
- Itm a comunion coppe (cup) of silver withe a cover.
- Itm a beriall cloth of red velvet and a pulpitte clothe of the same.
- Itm two grene velvet quishins (cushions).
- Itm a blewe velvet cope.
- Itm a blewe silke cope.
- Itm a white lynnen abe (albe) and a hedd clothe (amice) to the same.
- Itm a vestment of tawney velvet.
- Itm a vestment of redd rought velvet.
- Itm a vestment of grene silke with a crosse garde of red velvet.
- Itm a crosse banner of redd tafata gilted.
- Itm two stoles of redd velvet.
- Itm two white surplices.
- Itm two comunion table clothers.
- Itm two comunion towels.
- Itm one olde bible.
- Itm one great booke.
- Itm one olde sarvice booke for the minister."

APPENDIX IV

THE ORGAN

The organ now at St. Bartholomew's, where it supersedes one purchased by subscription in 1731, was originally built by George England in 1760 for the Church of St. Stephen, Walbrook. Considerable work was there done upon it by Messrs. William Hill and Son in 1872, viz:

    I.   The pipes of Great and Choir stops were replanted, CC pipes over the GG grooves, and the compass altered to CC to G throughout.

    II.   The following alterations were made in the Great organ:

Open Diapason (ii) extended from gamut G to CC.
Mixture replaced by new pipes where required.
New Trumpet inserted, and the old one transferred to Swell.

Choir.   Dulciana (new) C (grooved).
Keraulophon (new) C (grooved).
Clarinet CC.

Swell.   New soundboard (CC to G), swell-box and new action.
New Bourdon, 16 feet.
Cornet made into 12 and 15 feet.
New mixture—four ranks.
German Flute revoiced.
Old Great organ Trumpet arranged to form Double Trumpet from tenor C.
All stops, except German Flute and Double Trumpet, carried down to CC.

Pedal.   Bourdon, new, 16 feet.
Open Diapason, 16 feet (compass arranged CCC to F thirty notes).
Trombone, new, 16 feet

Couplers. New, Swell to Great, Great to Pedal, Swell to Pedal, Choir to Pedal, Swell to Choir.
New keyboards.

New Pedal keyboard.
New Drawstop knobs.
New additional bellows.
Five new Composition Pedals (three to Great organ, and
two to Swell organ).

81

Specification of the instrument after the above-mentioned work was
done.

Great Organ, CC to G.

Open Diapason (i)	8	feet
Open Diapason (ii)	8	"
Stopped Diapason	8	"
Principal	4	"
Twelfth	$2\,2/3$	"
Fifteenth	2	"
Nason Flute	4	"
Furniture.		
Sesquialtra.		
Trumpet	8	"
Clarion	8	"

Swell Organ, CC to G.

Bourdon	16	feet
Open Diapason	8	"
German Flute	8	"
Stopped Diapason	8	"
Principal	4	"
Twelfth	$2\,2/3$	"
Fifteenth	2	"
Double Trumpet (C)	16	"
Trumpet	8	"

| Oboe | 8 | " |
| Clarion | 4 | " |

Choir Organ, CC to G.

Dulciana	8	feet
Keraulophon (C grooved) 8		"
Stopped Diapason	8	"
Principal	4	"
Flute	4	"
Fifteenth	2	"
French Horn tenor F#	8	"
Vox Humana	8	"
Clarinet	8	"

Pedal Organ, CCC to F.

Open Diapason	16	feet
Bourdon	16	"
Trombone	16	"

Couplers.

Swell to Great.

Swell to Choir.

Swell to Pedal.

Great to Pedal.

Choir to Pedal.

Three Composition Pedals to Great.

Two Composition Pedals to Swell.

In 1886 the organ was purchased from St. Stephen's, Walbrook, for St. Bartholomew-the-Great, where a new case was made for it, the original being retained at St. Stephen's, for the sake of the carving, attributed to the famous Grinling Gibbons. Several alterations were then made in the instrument to adapt it to its new position, and at the present time the specification is as follows:

Great Organ, CC to G.

Open Diapason (i)	8	feet
Open Diapason (ii)	8	"
Stopped Diapason	8	"
Principal	4	"
Wald-Flute	4	"
Twelfth	$2\,2/3$	"
Fifteenth	2	"
Mixture (4 ranks).		
Furniture (3 ranks).		
Trumpet	8	"
Clarion	4	"

Swell Organ, CC to G.

Bourdon	16	feet
Open Diapason	8	"
German Flute	8	"
Stopped Diapason	8	"
Vox Angelica	8	"
Principal	4	"
Fifteenth	2	"
Mixture (4 ranks).		
Double Trumpet	16	"
Trumpet	8	"
Oboe	8	"
Clarion	4	"

Choir Organ, CC to G.

Dulciana	8	feet
Keraulophon	8	"

Hohl Flute	8	"
Gamba	8	"
Suabe Flute	4	"
Fifteenth	2	"
French Horn	8	"
Clarinet	8	"
Vox Humana	8	"

Pedal Organ, CCC to F.

Open Diapason	16	feet
Bourdon	16	"
Trombone	16	"

Couplers.

Swell to Great.
Swell to Choir.
Great to Pedal.
Choir to Pedal.
Swell to Pedal.

Five Combination Pedals.
Table of
Contents
83

DIMENSIONS OF THE CHURCH OF ST. BARTHO-LOMEW-THE-GREAT

(Internal)

		feet		inches
Choir:	Length	105	2	
	Breadth	27 "	8 "	
Ambulatory: Breadth		12 "	10 "	
Nave (surviving bay): From east to west		8 "	3 "	
North Transept:	From east to west	27 "	8 "	
	From north to south	19 "	3 "	
South Transept:	From east to west	27 "	4 "	
	From north to south	21 "	6 "	
Lady Chapel:	Length	60 "	6 "	
	Breadth	23 "	7 "	
Cloister (three bays restored):	Length	38 "	8 "	
	Breadth	13 "	2 "	

85

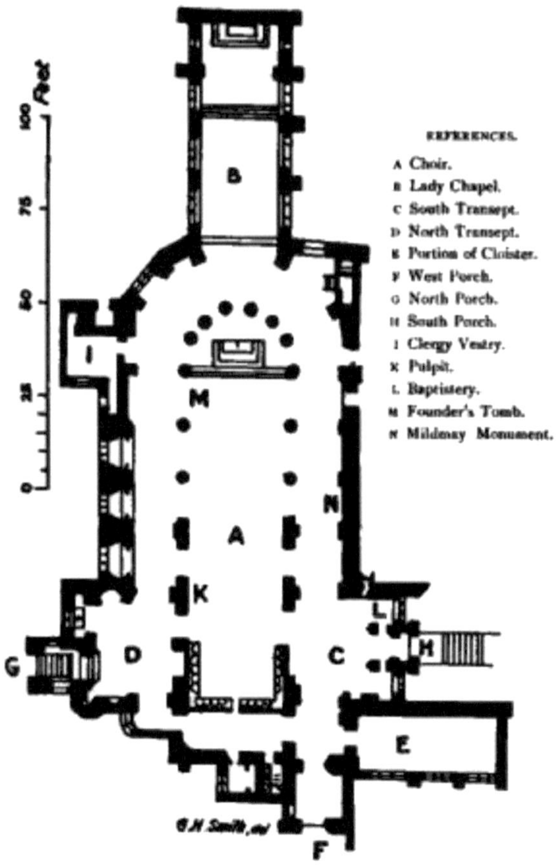

PLAN OF ST. BARTHOLOMEW-THE-GREAT (EXISTING CHURCH)

PLAN OF ST. BARTHOLOMEW-THE-GREAT (EXISTING CHURCH)

Opinions of the Press.

"For the purpose at which they aim they are admirably done, and there are few visitants to any of our noble shrines who will not enjoy their visit the better for being furnished with one of these delightful books, which can be slipped into the pocket and carried with ease, and is yet distinct and legible.... A volume such as that on Canterbury is exactly what we want, and on our next visit we hope to have it with us. It is thoroughly helpful, and the views of the fair city and its noble cathedral are beautiful. Both volumes, moreover, will serve more than a temporary purpose, and are trustworthy as well as delightful." — *Notes and Queries.*

"We have so frequently in these columns urged the want of cheap, well-illustrated, and well-written handbooks to our cathedrals, to take the place of the out-of-date publications of local booksellers, that we are glad to hear that they have been taken in hand by Messrs. George Bell & Sons." — *St. James's Gazette.*

"The volumes are handy in size, moderate in price, well illustrated, and written in a scholarly spirit. The history of cathedral and city is intelligently set forth and accompanied by a descriptive survey of the building in all its detail. The illustrations are copious and well selected, and the series bids fair to become an indispensable companion to the cathedral tourist in England." — *Times.*

"They are nicely produced in good type, on good paper, and contain numerous illustrations, are well written, and very cheap. We should imagine architects and students of architecture will be sure to buy the series as they appear, for they contain in brief much valuable information." — *British Architect.*

"Bell's 'Cathedral Series,' so admirably edited, is more than a description of the various English cathedrals. It will be a valuable historical record, and a work of much service also to the architect. The illustrations are well selected, and in many cases not mere bald architectural drawings but reproductions of exquisite stone fancies, touched in their treatment by fancy and guided by art." — *Star.*

"Each of them contains exactly that amount of information which the intelligent visitor, who is not a specialist, will wish to have. The disposition of the various parts is judiciously proportioned, and the style is very readable. The illustrations supply a further important feature; they are both numerous and good. A series which cannot fail to be welcomed by all who are interested in the ecclesiastical buildings of England." — *Glasgow Herald.*

"Those who, either for purposes of professional study or for a cultured recreation, find it expedient to 'do' the English cathedrals will welcome the beginning of Bell's 'Cathedral Series.' This set of books is an attempt to consult, more closely, and in greater detail than the usual guide-books do, the needs of visitors to the cathedral towns. The series cannot but prove markedly successful. In each book a business-like description is given of the fabric of the church to which the volume relates, and an interesting history of the relative diocese. The books are plentifully illustrated, and are thus made attractive as well as instructive. They cannot but prove welcome to all classes of readers interested either in English Church history or in ecclesiastical architecture." — *Scotsman.*

"They have nothing in common with the almost invariably wretched local guides save portability, and their only competitors in the quality and quantity of their contents are very expensive and mostly rare works, each of a size that suggests a packing-case rather than a coat-pocket. The 'Cathedral Series' are important compilations concerning history, architecture, and biography, and quite popular enough for such as take any sincere interest in their subjects." — *Sketch.*